DESIGN in 5

Essential Phases to Create Engaging Assessment Practice

Nicole Dimich Vagle

Solution Tree | Press

a division of
Solution Tree

555 North Morton Street
Bloomington, IN 47404
800.733.6786 (toll free) / 812.336.7700
FAX: 812.336.7790

email: info@solution-tree.com
solution-tree.com

Visit **go.solution-tree.com/assessment** to download the reproducibles in this book.

Printed in the United States of America

18   17   16   6   7   8   9   10

Library of Congress Cataloging-in-Publication Data

Dimich Vagle, Nicole.
 Design in five : essential phases to create engaging assessment practice / Nicole Dimich Vagle.
    pages cm.
 Includes bibliographical references and index.
  ISBN 978-1-936764-95-2 (perfect bound) 1. Educational tests and measurements. 2. Educational evaluation. 3. Motivation in education. 4. Effective teaching. I. Title.
  LB3051.D538 2014
  371.26--dc23
                         2014021737

Solution Tree
Jeffrey C. Jones, CEO
Edmund M. Ackerman, President

Solution Tree Press
President: Douglas M. Rife
Associate Acquisitions Editor: Kari Gillesse
Editorial Director: Lesley Bolton
Managing Production Editor: Caroline Weiss
Senior Production Editor: Edward M. Levy
Proofreader: Ashante K. Thomas
Text and Cover Designer: Rian Anderson
Text Compositor: Rachel Smith

To Maya, Rhys, and Chase
May your school experiences be filled with rich and meaningful
learning that inspires you to wonder, grow, and persevere.

Acknowledgments

Thank you to educators all over who have participated in my training sessions, offered reflections on my work, loaned me moments in classrooms, invited me to team meetings, and shared successes, challenges, and questions. The ideas in this book stand on the shoulders of all of those amazing educators, from whom I have learned so much.

Thank you, in particular, to Jen Kunze, whom I have had the pleasure of teaming with in more assessment sessions than I can count and to Cassie Erkens for your partnership and unending belief in me. Also to Kalli-ann Binkowski, Missey Chavez, Wendy Eggermont, Kathy Glass, Joanne Harmsen, Tammy Heflebower, Amy Ladue, Angela LaBounty, Jeff Ronneberg, Phil Schlechty, Ken Simon, Jim Smith, Jane Stevenson, and Denise Waalen for being the incredible educators you are—committed to engaging students and empowering teachers. You each have taken time to review a draft or have a conversation that has pushed my thinking and helped the ideas in this book take shape.

With special gratitude to my family—to Mark for your love and support in looking at drafts and listening to me share and wrestle with ideas; to my parents, Tom and Judy Dimich, who have supported me unconditionally and watched and cared for their grandchildren on countless occasions; and to Jeanne Johnson and Dennis and Sheila Vagle, who have also shown me incredible support. These wonderful grandparents have spent lots of time with their grandchildren and helped make this book possible.

Without the support, inspiration, encouragement, and perseverance of Claudia Wheatley and Douglas Rife, this book would not have happened. I am indebted to you for your unwavering support and belief in my work.

To Lesley Bolton and Ed Levy, I am incredibly grateful for your review, editing, revisions, and insights. You have made these ideas come to life in writing, and your patience and perseverance are unmatched.

With humble gratitude, I submit this work to the field for dialogue, critique, and inspiration.

Solution Tree Press would like to thank the following reviewers:

Julie Brua
Assistant Superintendent of Curriculum and
  Instruction
Aptakisic-Tripp School District 102
Buffalo Grove, Illinois

Forrest Clark
Eighth-Grade Math Teacher
Nisqually Middle School
Lacey, Washington

Cassandra Erkens
Education Consultant
Lakeville, Minnesota

Jim Knight
Fourth-Grade Teacher
Pearl S. Buck Elementary School
Levittown, Pennsylvania

Jon Moore
Eleventh- and Twelfth-Grade English Teacher
Shepherd High School
Shepherd, Montana

Erik Powell
Grades 9–12 English Language Arts Teacher
Joel E. Ferris High School
Spokane, Washington

Jeanne Spiller
Assistant Superintendent of Teaching & Learning,
  Curriculum & Instruction
Kildeer Countryside Community Consolidated
  School District 96
Buffalo Grove, Illinois

Visit **go.solution-tree.com/assessment** to download
reproducibles and access live links from this book.

Table of Contents

Reproducible pages are in italics.

About the Author

 Nicole Dimich Vagle's passion for education and lifelong learning has led her to extensively explore, facilitate, and implement innovative practices in school transformation. She works with elementary and secondary educators in presentations, trainings, and consultations in the spirit of providing students with engaging and inspiring learning experiences.

As a middle and high school English teacher, Nicole teamed with math, social studies, and science teachers. Pursuing her belief in the powerful impact teacher leaders have in schools and districts, she later became a program evaluator and trainer at the Center for Supportive Schools (formerly known as the Princeton Center for Leadership Training) in Princeton, New Jersey.

Nicole partners with Spring Lake Park Schools in Minnesota, where she supports the design of engaging and rigorous instruction and assessment in elementary, middle, and high schools. She has produced a training DVD that illustrates a protocol for examining the effectiveness of assessments and student learning and continues to work with schools and districts nationwide to increase their understanding of developing and using assessments to promote student learning and engagement. A featured presenter at conferences throughout North America, Nicole empowers educators to build capacity for and implement engaging assessment design, formative assessment practices, common assessment design and analysis, data-driven decisions, student-work protocols, and motivational strategies.

Nicole is the coauthor of *Motivating Students: 25 Strategies to Light the Fire of Engagement*. She is also the author of two chapters in assessment anthologies—"Inspiring and Requiring Learning" in *Teacher as Assessment Leader* and "Finding Meaning in the Numbers" in *Principal as Assessment Leader*.

Nicole earned a bachelor of arts in English and psychology from Concordia College in Moorhead, Minnesota, and a master of arts in human development from Saint Mary's University of Minnesota in Minneapolis. She and her husband, Mark, have three children, Maya, Rhys, and Chase, and live in Minnetonka, Minnesota.

To book Nicole Dimich Vagle for professional development, contact pd@solution-tree.com.

Foreword

By Douglas Reeves

Standards come and go, but assessment is what matters for students, parents, and teachers. In this thoughtful and challenging book, Nicole Dimich Vagle demystifies assessment and provides a road map for educators who want to connect with their students with intellectually challenging and personally engaging work. Backed by impressive research and personal experience, Vagle leads us through a five-step process beginning with standards and continuing through reporting the results. Long after the Common Core State Standards and other standards have been revised, rejected, and reinvented, Vagle's work will provide teachers, administrators, students, and parents with the intellectual discipline and consistency that are essential for improvement. Politicians can debate endlessly about the *what* of education, but this book reminds us that the *how*—essentials of effective teaching, assessment, and feedback practices—will endure.

Perhaps the most important words in this book are *student investment*. Consider how strikingly different this phrase is from the terror and intimidation that students so frequently associate with assessments. Rather than seeing assessment as the final stage of the learning process, this book makes clear that a process of feedback, goal setting, revision, and improvement is the key to the constructive use of assessment. The author reminds us that assessment need not be an instrument associated with threats but rather can be, like the baton of the music teacher, a way of encouraging, nudging, and ultimately achieving better results from students and educators.

School administrators should take particular note of Vagle's balanced approach to assessment. These pages make clear that performance assessment and selected-response assessment are not warring camps but complementary methods to assess student performance. And while rubrics have been in vogue for more than two decades, our profession must confront the stark division between rubrics that are specific and helpful and those that are vague and subjective. Although I've written hundreds of rubrics, this book made me rethink my own instructional practices with an endeavor to improve the clarity and quality of every rubric that I use with students, teachers, and educational leaders.

Prepare to be challenged by the advice in this book about the reporting of student work. Perhaps the most controversial words you will read are, "Report work habits separately from student achievement." This advice, while completely sound and consistent with the best research on grading and reporting, flies in the face of contemporary computerized grading practices. In too many schools around the world, every missed assignment is calculated as a zero and therefore dooms students to failure, even if they respond positively to teacher feedback and improve their work. In these systems, the sins at the beginning of the semester continue to be punished months later. Those who believe that grading is fundamentally a system of punishment and rewards will not find this attractive, but I hope that skeptics will be open-minded to the research-based approach that Vagle offers.

I particularly appreciate the willingness of the author and publisher to make available reproducible handouts, something that makes this book an ideal faculty book study. This is not a book merely to be read, but to be *used*. When you are finished, it should be full of highlights, underlines, and torn pages. The author invites readers to be co-creators, reflecting on their personal experiences and professional practices. That is a refreshing and welcome change from expert opinion that allows for little conversation or collegial discussion.

It is a rare book that can reach such a wide audience and broad range of grade levels, from prekindergarten to high school. Nicole Dimich Vagle has accomplished this, and readers will be grateful for her efforts.

Douglas Reeves, PhD, is the author of more than thirty books, including Elements of Grading: A Guide to Effective Practice, *and editor of* Ahead of the Curve: The Power of Assessment to Transform Teaching and Learning. *He was named a Brock International Laureate for his contributions to education and received the Contribution to the Field Award from the National Staff Development Council. His most recent research can be found at ChangeLeaders.com.*

Introduction

Children have "an instinct of workmanship"—a built-in desire to do work
they love very carefully. It is the task of schooling to engage and nurture that
"instinct" to help children learn at their best.

—John Holt

My son Rhys is a thinker. Mechanically inclined, he loves to build, create, and analyze how things are put together, and he will wear anyone out with his questions. When Rhys was in preschool, his teachers regularly found him trying to climb onto the trash can in the bathroom. After many days of repeat offenses and consequences, an astute assistant teacher recognized Rhys's motivation. Apparently, the paper-towel dispenser broke regularly throughout the day. Attempting to repair it, Rhys was trying to reach a key that was required to access the dispenser. Once this was discovered, the assistant teacher worked with him on the dispenser—or as she put it, she watched Rhys figure out how to make it work. From that moment forward, Rhys became the go-to guy to fix the paper-towel dispenser.

When assessments are designed well and information is used effectively, this kind of engagement can be fostered in each classroom, creating a culture in which student work is meaningful and arises out of a consideration of who our students are, how they learn, and what conditions will encourage them to invest in the communities that we have designed to help them grow. In high-quality assessment practices, teachers design, use, and respond to assessment information in ways that build strong relationships and a classroom culture focused on learning—one that empowers students to invest. High-quality assessment practices:

- Motivate and engage students
- Communicate strengths in terms of learning
- Provide intentional opportunities to learn from mistakes and failure
- Generate confidence and success

Assessment Defined

Assessment is an intentional process of gathering information, both formal and informal, to understand a student's learning and performance in order to facilitate and communicate achievement and levels of proficiency. In Rhys's case, the information was obtained informally through observation and conversation and used to facilitate learning and engagement. The teacher obtained insight into how to help Rhys learn and engage more productively and made changes accordingly. The Latin root of *assessment, assidere,* means to "sit beside." The notion of "sitting beside" a student in order to gather information to inform and inspire action is different than evaluation, when the information is used to make a judgment about a level of proficiency, to communicate achievement at that moment in time, or determine the effectiveness of a program. Gathering the information is the first part of a high-quality assessment practice. Using it well is the next part.

Using assessment well means capitalizing on the information collected and using those insights to facilitate learning and foster hope for students. When students see their work in terms of their strengths and what they understand, and see deficits as opportunities to grow, assessment provides more information about how to get better. Starting from a place of strength creates a culture that honors where students are and *expects* that all students will grow. Dylan Wiliam (2011) describes another view of motivation in his book *Embedded Formative Assessment*: "There is another way to think about motivation—not as a cause but as a consequence of achievement" (p. 149). When students see hope and possibility, they are much more willing to engage, persevere, and achieve.

Assessment has become an integral part of evaluating high-quality educational practices and informing the most effective next steps in students achieving more. In a balanced assessment system, there are multiple types of assessments that serve an intentionally designed purpose. If we gather the information but never stop to analyze it or use it in the way it was intended, we can create a lot of additional work for students and teachers. Table I.1 describes common types of assessments and their most beneficial purpose. Identify the specific types of assessments that you use. How is each assessment used by teachers, students, teams, district and school leadership, families, and the community? Which data are used to inform versus evaluate? How much energy and time is spent on each type of assessment? When teachers and students spend more time and energy on the types of assessment at the top half of the graph (standardized, benchmark, end-of-course assessment, and even summative assessment), the tendency is to feel overwhelmed, with a sense of no time to teach or help students learn. Those data are further away from the classroom and often don't build in time for an instructional response that can influence student learning. In some cases, they are not designed for that purpose. Standardized assessment data are not meant to inform instruction on a daily basis. They are designed to evaluate the effectiveness of the overall instructional program at a particular school. When gaps in achievement are identified, we do not do more standardized assessment; instead, teachers and teams check in with students using common and ongoing formative assessment to be able to respond to misconceptions and help students grow. This kind of assessment information has the biggest influence on student learning, as it is about identifying what students understand and what they need to move forward, and it is about taking action to improve. Instruction is then planned based on this information. Students move and grow the most when responses occur in an ongoing basis. Summative assessments need to be designed well and reflect learning on standards. The majority of a teacher's time in individual and team planning, however, should be spent using common and ongoing formative assessment to plan instruction. Analyzing formative data should be seen as integral to lesson planning—not as an additional task. A balanced assessment system provides all stakeholders with important information about student learning. An effective system pays attention to different types of assessment and uses the information for its intended purpose.

Summative assessments, which are used to communicate proficiency and progress at a moment in time, are roughly synonymous with *evaluation*. It is a situation in which one is making a judgment. Assigning a mark, grade, or percentage is common practice in summative assessment. This, in itself, is not negative, but problems do occur when schools send mixed or confusing messages to students, parents, and families about what that mark, grade, or percentage means and how it will be used, often resulting in a culture focused on marks or gathering points, rather than improving, learning, and growing. For example, when we average all scores together and don't take in to consideration the growth that has occurred during instruction, the grade is a fuzzy indicator of what students knew before and how much growth they have achieved. (Chapter 5 will dig deeper into some key issues of grading and how to effectively communicate student learning in both formative and summative ways.)

Table I.1: The Purpose and Types of Assessment

Assessment Format	Best Use of Information
Standardized Tests	School or district-leadership, department, or grade-level teams use this information to evaluate the effectiveness of a program, structure, or curriculum or to consider the level of proficiency of groups of students. They are usually administered only once (in some places twice) a year so the data can be used to consider how to change curriculum and general instructional practices for the following year, including what perhaps to emphasize as a system. Unless teachers are examining standardized assessment data of current students, and have time to respond, data only reflect the effectiveness of past instruction and curriculum. Analyzing the previous year's standardized data on current students, if available, may help focus instruction or assessment practice, but the more time that passes between when the test was administered and when action is taken, the less accurate the information for influencing individual student learning. Analyzing these data is about evaluation and general program effectiveness. These aren't data that tightly inform instruction.
District Benchmark Assessments	Districts and schools use this information most often to determine progress toward student achievement on the standardized test. Sometimes schools use these data to identify individual students who need additional time and support. In this case, data are used to appropriately place students in intervention programs. Teachers can use these data to determine progress and plan how to focus units of instruction in teams or individually. These assessments are usually administered three to four times a year—the more immediate the results, the more impact the data can have on instruction and student learning. Data should be analyzed and shared within a week or two. The more time passes before results are analyzed, the less accurate the data become and the less able teachers are to use it to respond to student learning needs. If results take longer, the analysis and response are more challenging. More school-focused data may be collected to assess if students' understanding has changed.
End-of-Course Assessments	Districts use these assessments to ensure equity and alignment to standards. School leadership examines these data to determine the effectiveness of curriculum and instruction. Teachers analyze these data to determine the effectiveness of the assessment and make any necessary curriculum changes that need to occur in the following year. These assessments are administered one to two times per year, depending on the length of the course.

Continued on next page →

Summative Assessments (Common or Individual)	Department, grade-level teams, or individual teachers analyze these data at a moment when they expect students to have already learned the intended content. Teachers may examine an example of student work generated from the assessment to address any gaps in learning and to evaluate the assessment itself.
	These are administered as often as students are expected to have learned something and when that learning will be quantified in terms of a grade, rubric score, or proficiency level (sometimes described as a standards-based mark).
	If analysis happens immediately and teachers discover gaps in understanding that are essential for students to understand in order to be successful in the future, they may choose to spend a few extra days on the intended learning. If used in this way, it is now formative, not summative.
	Or, teachers may decide that the intended learning will occur again in a future unit.
	Or, teachers may decide it isn't essential and will modify curriculum and instruction to be more effective the following year.
Common Formative Assessments	Teams of teachers use these data to check in with students about their progress in achieving an essential learning outcome. Teams identify the essential-to-know, hard-to-learn, and hard-to-teach concepts and plan to gather information on these essential learning goals. Individual students in need of support or advancement are identified based on their strengths and areas of growth. Interventions and responses are planned in teams to meet the immediate learning needs of students.
	Both students and teachers use this data to inform next steps in student learning. The teacher plans a response that addresses the gaps in learning or deepens the learning.
	Students reflect on what the assessment data tell them about their strengths, their intended learning, and their next steps in that learning (goal setting).
	If teams meet weekly, it is possible to administer, analyze, and respond every three to four weeks. If teams meet daily, analysis can occur perhaps every one to two weeks.
	If teams meet monthly, analysis can occur perhaps two to three times per year. The instructional response is essential if common formative assessments are to improve achievement.
Formative Assessments	Individual teachers use both informal and formal assessment information to make decisions in the moment or day to day. Because teachers are responding to students' understanding and misconceptions immediately, this is where the most change in learning happens (Wiliam, 2011). The other types of assessment help emphasize what is important for students to learn. It is the response in these moments that fosters the biggest hope and possibility of achieving more.
	Sometimes called assessment for learning, with formative assessment, both teachers and students are working hard to address misconceptions and grow more.

Source: Adapted from Vagle, 2009a.

Formative assessment, used by teachers and students to make decisions about next steps and about how students might grow and improve, is an ongoing process. Students make revisions in response to feedback, teachers plan discussions based on intriguing questions, students fix errors, and teachers provide minilessons based on misconceptions found in student work or heard in student dialogue, so that students can continue to work and revise their work.

Both summative and formative assessments can take the form of tests, papers, quizzes, projects, weblogs, informal and formal observations, dialogues, presentations, or any other process through which we gather information about a student's learning and understanding. While the table indicates formative and summative assessment types, it is how they are used that makes them this way. In a balanced system, teachers have planned intentional evidence or student work (summative assessments) to show proficiency on a particular set of learning goals. Teachers intentionally plan moments for students to practice and revise (formative assessment) prior to these summative assessments. In an effective system, assessment and evaluation work together to promote learning, communicate progress, and report achievement.

When assessment is strength based, students gain information, sometimes in the form of written or verbal feedback, about where they are. From their assessment information, teachers structure reflection, feedback, and activities so students start to see connections between what they are learning and what they are doing. Students learn and reflect on their strengths in terms of what they understand, or what they know and can do, not just through a grade, percentage, or smiley face. Such assessments naturally promote a growth mindset—students come to believe that if they put effort toward something, they will learn more and improve. With a fixed mindset, students don't see a relationship between the work they put forth and their improvement. In fact, they don't believe that any effort they put forth will help them improve or develop a deeper understanding (Dweck, 2006). Nan Henderson (2013) captured the power of building on strengths through the kind of messages from teachers that builds resilience in students: "I see what is right with you, despite your struggles. And I believe what is right with you is more powerful than anything that is wrong" (p. 22). When students see their strengths, this type of resilience can be built through our assessment practices.

Effective assessment also provides intentional opportunities to learn how to learn from mistakes and failure in ways that produce confidence and success. All too often, students (and sometimes teachers and parents) perceive mistakes as evidence that they aren't good enough or as a sign of a character flaw. When students see assessment in terms of deficits rather than opportunities, their self-confidence plummets and their hope fades. The often-expressed feeling "I don't care" or "This is stupid" may really mean "I don't know" or "I'm frustrated." Take, for example, a student who earned a 63 percent on an assessment. That student is probably not feeling very confident about her understanding. But that overall score does not communicate much about learning or point that student toward improvement. Now look at the same score broken down for that student by learning goal (figure I.1).

Sahira Jones	Number of Correct Items
I can organize data collected from a survey question into a chart or graph.	10/10
I can calculate measures of central tendency from a data set.	8/10
I can interpret my data. This means I can draw conclusions about data.	1/10
Overall Score	**63 percent (19/30)**

Figure I.1: Fifth-grade score broken down by learning goal.

Communicating assessment information like this is a game changer for students. Sahira can now see exactly what that 63 percent means: she is solid in organizing data and proficient in calculating measures of central tendency (if 80 percent is proficient), and she needs to work on interpreting data. Both teachers and students benefit from this information. Sahira can now say, "I have met two out of three goals. I have one to go." Starting from a place of strength and providing specific information to improve creates a sense of hope and direction. When students see a pathway to improve, their confidence increases and they will be more likely to invest energy without coercion. Teachers will need to require students to address and learn from mistakes (and build this type of analysis into their instruction). And when students do learn from those mistakes and see growth, both in terms of their score and their learning, the seeds of motivation and engagement through high-quality assessment practice are planted.

About This Book

This book is about intentionally designing engaging, rigorous, and meaningful assessments and using information we derive from them to empower students to invest and fully engage in their learning. It is about empowering teachers to create and use assessments that reflect meaningful work—work that sets students up for success in their future coursework and helps them make productive choices, learn from failure, and persevere to achieve their goals. Engaging assessment practices happen in a culture focused on learning and trust, where students and teachers are working to build strong relationships through meaningful and rigorous work.

Engaging assessment practices happen in a culture focused on learning and trust, where students and teachers are working to build strong relationships through meaningful and rigorous work.

Depending on where you are in the journey, some of the ideas in this book will affirm the practices you are already doing, while others will hopefully take your work a step further. Each teacher, team, school, district, state, and province must consider its situation and begin a conversation about quality assessment. My hope is that this book will contribute to those conversations.

This introduction is followed by six chapters and an appendix. The remainder of the introduction discusses assessment design qualities, and the phases of an assessment design process that I have named Design in Five. Chapters 1 through 5 are devoted to the five phases of Design in Five.

- **Phase one:** Choosing standards and planning engagement
- **Phase two:** Analyzing the standards and sketching out learning goals
- **Phase three:** Crafting an assessment plan
- **Phase four:** Creating the assessment and gathering the materials
- **Phase five:** Determining student investment and the reporting method

Chapter 6 discusses how to work with the Design in Five process in collaboration, whether you are in a professional learning community or some other team-based form of organization in your school. At the end of each chapter, a Pause and Ponder section offers some guiding questions for reflecting on the ideas put forward in that chapter. These may be used as study guides to generate dialogue and action for either individuals or groups.

An appendix contains reproducible forms of many of the tables, charts, and other resources in this book. You may also visit **go.solution-tree.com/assessment**, where you can download these and numerous other resources, including examples gathered from around the globe that will prompt your own ideas about how to revise and deepen assessment work. See page 129 for a list of additional resources and page 131 for a list of examples of assessment work found online to prompt your own ideas.

Assessment Design Qualities

My synthesis of assessment design qualities—standards that provide the foundation for effective and engaging assessment design and use—is based on the work of many amazing educators, including Jan Chappuis, Anne Davies, Cassandra Erkens, John Hattie, Tammy Heflebower, Robert J. Marzano, Milbrey McLaughlin, Ken O'Connor, James W. Popham, Thomas R. Guskey, Douglas Reeves, Phil Schlechty, Rick Stiggins, Joan Talbert, and Dylan Wiliam. Following are the three primary design characteristics that I have derived from their work and my own.

1. Designing with precision

2. Employing effective action

3. Fostering student investment

Designing With Precision

Designing with precision begins with selecting and describing what we intend students to learn and then determining a method, or type of student work that will give students and teachers information about the extent to which they have done so.

Selecting and Describing Learning

Many schools, districts, and jurisdictions have approached the process of defining learning goals by unpacking (Ainsworth, 2003) and deconstructing standards (Stiggins, Arter, Chappuis, & Chappuis, 2004). In essence, teachers identify the knowledge and skills needed to achieve the standard. In this analysis of the standard, teachers consider the cognitive level (the thinking students need to do, such as recall, apply, synthesize, and create) required to achieve the standard and beyond. Phase two in Design in Five addresses how to choose learning goals for assessments. There are various documents and resources that help teachers define and interpret the standards, but no matter what documents we have at our fingertips, teachers must still work with colleagues to make meaning of the learning goals and determine the kind of student work that will best reflect achievement. That leads to the second part of designing with precision, determining the method.

Determining the Method

A method is the work students produce that provides information about a student's thinking and learning. We may ask students to produce a video, write a weblog, conduct an interview, create a Prezi presentation, take a multiple-choice test, or write a paper. Each type of method has strengths and limitations regarding the effectiveness and efficiency of getting high-quality information about student learning. Let's take, for example, this literacy standard in the National Governors Association Center for Best Practices and Council of Chief State School Officers' ([NGA & CCSSO] 2010a) Common Core State Standards.

> **RST.11–12.7:** Integrate and evaluate multiple sources of information presented in diverse formats and media (e.g., quantitative data, video, multimedia) in order to address a question or solve a problem. (p. 62)

Suppose a physics teacher asks students to (1) read an account of the meteor that hit Russia in February 2013, (2) read a follow-up research report on the event, and (3) watch a video of a scientist explaining the phenomenon. If the assessment method is multiple-choice or short-answer questions asking students to identify the main points made in each of the two texts and the video, the assessment will help the teacher understand if students got the gist of what the texts were saying. However, it will be difficult to tell if students have, as the standard describes, integrated and evaluated multiple sources of information because the test questions only allow students to show their literal understanding. The standard asks student to *integrate* and *evaluate* when addressing a question or solving a problem. In order for the method to address this standard, the assessment would need to ask students to decide what information from the articles was most useful to address a problem. For example, a task that asked students to consider what information from these articles could best be used to predict future meteorites, and then write a letter to scientists describing their thinking, would require students to integrate what they understood from the article and evaluate evidence that could contribute to solving the problem of predicting future meteorites. That type of student work would be most effective in understanding the extent to which students achieved the targeted standard.

To take another example, a third-grade team's assessment involves identifying the adjectives in various sentences. Let's take a look at the third-grade standard in the Common Core regarding adjectives.

> **L.3.1g:** Form and use comparative and superlative adjectives and adverbs, and choose between them depending on what is to be modified. (NGA & CCSSO, 2010a, p. 28)

The standard calls for students to form and use adjectives, which means that students need to do more than identify. Multiple-choice items cannot provide the opportunity to demonstrate this learning goal, because students are simply selecting a word. Asking students to underline the adjectives in a sentence or to choose the adjective from a list of options requires identifying, but not forming or using. A more effective method, which captures the essence of the standard, would ask students to use comparative and superlative adjectives in context or to communicate or describe a situation effectively in which they were comparing two or more things or situations. The method might involve showing students two pictures and asking them to write about how the pictures are similar and different using comparative and superlative adjectives (for example, *tall, taller, tallest; happy, happier, happiest*). This points to one of the most essential aspects of assessment design—matching the verb in the learning goals (in this case, *form* and *use*) to the method of assessment in order to get accurate evidence of student understanding (Stiggins et al., 2004).

Some might ask, "Shouldn't we be getting our students used to standardized test formats?" It is unnecessary and counterproductive to shape the form of every assessment to reflect that of a standardized test. While students need some practice in taking these types of tests, too much practice can lead to bored students who are disengaged and who fail to see how their schooling is preparing them for future success (Allensworth, Correa, & Ponisciak, 2008). In fact, research suggests that using the method of the standardized test frequently does not equate to higher levels of achievement (Wiliam, 2013). When a student asks that classic question, "Why do we have to do this?" the answer has to be more than "Because it will be on the test." In a balanced assessment system, some time is devoted to practicing the standardized assessment method. The Purpose and Types of Assessment chart (table I.1, page 3) describes benchmark assessments administered two to three times a year that can aid with this preparation. Most classroom assessment is designed to gather high-quality information about students' understanding of the standards for the purpose of communicating achievement at a moment in time (grades or marks) or to inform instructional planning and inspire student growth. The form the assessment takes creates engagement and meaning for students. Using multiple methods over time, intentionally placed, is a hallmark of high-quality assessment practice. Using different types of methods signals to students the relevance, as well as the meaning, of their learning. Chapter 3 describes how to choose methods, along with the strengths and limitations of many different types of student work.

Accounting for Error

Error in assessment design and use occurs when student performance on an assessment can be attributed to something other than understanding of the learning the assessment was intended to address. The first potential error when designing with precision involves identifying potential for bias—that is, recognizing any assumed cultural and background knowledge students need to succeed. Every assessment makes inferences about a student's understanding. Making the wrong inferences due to unintentional bias or assumed background knowledge can lead to the wrong conclusions. A collaborative team I worked with examined results from a reading comprehension assessment for an article about geckos. All but one student did quite poorly. When the team asked this student what he thought contributed to his strong performance, he told them he used to live in Guam, where there were geckos crawling all over their walls. The goal of this assessment was to get a sense of students' reading comprehension, but in reality the assessment was gauging students' understanding and experience with geckos!

This assessment was intended to be formative. Teachers looked at the student responses and planned instruction for the next day. Given that the student who did well had background information, the team realized that the instruction needed in this situation was more about understanding of geckos. They focused the next day's classroom instruction around how to engage in a text that addresses a topic with which you do not have much experience. Students re-read the text and worked in pairs to revise their responses on the reading assessment. If the assessment had been summative, meaning teachers were intending to score it and use it as a grade or a mark to show the extent to which students could comprehend text, they would have needed to do another assessment once they had realized that background knowledge was the reason students did poorly. This assessment would not have described student's reading comprehension. Sometimes we don't realize the influence of factors like these on achievement until after the assessment; but once we do, we can revise the scoring or use the example as an instructional tool.

Vocabulary is the second type of error to consider, as it can also contribute to misleading assessment information if not intentionally taught and purposefully considered in the assessment design. For example, in science, independent and dependent variables are sometimes called *manipulating* and *responding* variables, respectively. If *manipulating* and *responding* are used in instruction and *independent* and *dependent* are used on the test, students may score poorly not because they do not understand the concept but because of the switched terminology. By being aware of terminology and vocabulary, you can sometimes avoid questions about the validity of the assessment results.

Employing Effective Action

The second of the three design qualities is employing effective action to use and communicate the information derived from assessment information. When a tight alignment exists between formative and summative assessments, there is enough time for students to practice and revise (using formative assessment) before being evaluated on the content, as well as sufficient evidence to communicate achievement (using summative assessment).

Using Assessment Formatively

Although research suggests that formative assessment has great potential to positively influence student learning (Black & Wiliam, 1998; Dunn & Mulvenon, 2009; Shepard, 2000; Wiliam, Lee, Harrison, & Black,

2004; Wininger, 2005), there is no universal agreement on an exact definition of formative assessment, which leads to a fuzzy picture of how to use assessment to inspire growth (Dunn & Mulvenon, 2009). Significant evidence, however, shows that specific aspects of formative assessment—using descriptive feedback, goal setting, involving students, and essentially, acting on information about student understanding—do support and improve student learning (Hattie, 2009; Hattie & Timperley, 2007; Marzano, 2006). As Wiliam (2011) describes, "Assessment functions formatively when it improves the instructional decisions that are made by teachers, learners, and peers. These decisions can be immediate, on-the-fly decisions or longer term" (p. 45). A key element of this definition is that action must be taken by teachers *and* learners for the purpose of improvement. Teachers use this information to plan instruction, turning the assessment into something that is forming next steps and lesson plans, but it is not just the adults in the situation who are informed and act on assessment information.

In formative assessment practices, when students receive detailed feedback that describes their strengths and next steps, they are required to act on that feedback or analyze their mistakes. It is this action of using the information to improve that makes the assessment formative. Descriptive feedback should lead to students being more independent and better able to assess and comment on their own work, thus sharing with teachers the responsibility of improving their work. Revision, mistake analysis, self-assessment, and goal setting—all are important components of formative assessment that employs effective action.

Using Assessment Summatively

Using assessment summatively means gathering information about the level of success or proficiency obtained at a moment when you *expect* students to have some level of proficiency on a standard or benchmark (often at the end of an instructional unit but sometimes along the way). Summative assessments can provide strong inferences about a student's performance at a particular moment in time and are most often reported by points, percentages, a rubric, or a standards-based score. But before summative evidence is collected and used to communicate proficiency, students must have opportunities to practice and improve.

To be effective, the reporting and grading practices associated with summative assessment must clearly communicate academic achievement separately from the evaluation of a student's behavior and work habits. Grades and standards-based reporting should be seen as a *system* (Guskey & Bailey, 2001, 2010), one in which student progress is communicated to families in a way that leaves ample time for students to improve before the end of the unit or before the quarterly, semester, or trimester report card. Chapter 5 describes effective grading practices that lead to communicating learning more effectively.

Employing effective action is about effectively communicating what the assessment means in terms of student learning and then structuring action based on that information. This is an essential aspect of using assessment to engage students in their learning. When students have more information about what they understand (their strengths) and what they need to do to get better (next steps, revision, mistakes), it gives them hope and power in being able to achieve more. This hope and power is the foundation for motivation and engagement.

Fostering Student Investment

The third design quality, fostering student investment, intentionally brings students in as partners in their learning. This means they clearly see and understand the connections among learning, homework, tests, instruction, grades, and improvement. With this information, students plan how to move their own learning forward. Students who are invested recognize when they feel confident as well as when they feel unsure. Their mistakes lead them to areas they need to study more, and teachers provide the structure and lessons to ensure that they do so.

Student investment is also built through seeking feedback from students. John Hattie (2009) discusses the power of teachers gathering feedback from students and using it to inform their instruction and assessment practices. In this practice, teachers may informally ask students the extent to which an instructional activity, feedback, or homework assignment influenced their learning or success. Teachers may more formally ask students to reflect on teaching or grading practices. Chapter 5 discusses at more length the type of student feedback teachers might use to inform their assessment practices.

I am intentionally using the word *investment* instead of *involvement* to signal a reciprocal relationship between student and teacher, one that leads to the student taking the reins and beginning to own and value his or her own learning. When students are invested, they:

- Have language to describe their learning
- Have a clear idea of quality and not-so-quality work
- Take action on descriptive feedback
- Revise their work
- Self-reflect on what the assessment means in terms of their learning
- Set goals based on assessment information
- Make an action plan in partnership with teachers to achieve their goals and improve
- Share their work and plans to improve
- Share their thoughts on what helps them learn and what gets in the way of their learning
- Experience the ways in which the learning is relevant and challenging through assessments, instructional activities, and homework that teachers design

Student investment happens in a culture focused on learning. To achieve a classroom where students are invested in their learning, all three design qualities must be intentionally at play. In order for students to invest, the learning must be described and students must see connections between their work and achievement (designing with precision). To invest, students must also experience times when they are practicing, getting feedback, and improving their work (employing action formatively), and then after this growth and improvement, when they see their grade or mark reflect that achievement (employing action summatively), investment begins to grow. As students experience this action, they begin to invest and are able to set meaningful goals and produce relevant work that engages them and creates a desire to want to succeed.

A useful, reproducible checklist, "Review Your Current Assessment With the Three Design Qualities," can be found on page 134, or visit **go.solution-tree.com/assessment** to download this resource.

The Design in Five Process

Design in Five is a process for developing effective, efficient, and engaging assessments that hold to the foundational beliefs and design qualities previously discussed. Based on my work with countless educators, this five-phase process produces meaningful assessments, empowers teachers, and creates assessment experiences that lead to quality evidence of learning.

The dialogue that occurs through the creation of assessment practices can be rich, messy, and incredibly meaningful as teachers work individually and together to create assessments that reflect student achievement and that are worth the time and paper (or the hard drive and Cloudspace). Assessment is as much about the process as it is the result. Consider why some people like to fish. Some find it relaxing and a great time to connect with family and friends. Others love the peacefulness and solitude, and many do enjoy the catch. However, there is a reason they didn't call fishing "catching." It is through the process, much like fishing, that we gain insight and inspiration. The actual catch, or assessment, is only one aspect of the work—the process is where meaning is made and engagement fostered. Educators work tremendously hard to create the best possible school and learning experiences for students. This protocol offers guidance to continue that work. Figure I.2 provides an overview of all five phases.

Phase One

1. Choose the standards.
2. Plan engagement.

Phase Two

1. Analyze the standards.
2. Sketch out the learning goals.

Phase Three

1. Identify the learning goals for the assessment.
2. Choose the method of assessment.
3. Determine the weight and number of items for each learning goal.

Phase Four

1. Create or revise assessment items and tasks for each learning goal.
2. Develop student documents and gather necessary materials.

Phase Five

1. Create a scoring scheme that reflects the learning.
2. Choose strategies to foster student investment.

Figure I.2: The Design in Five process.

Visit **go.solution-tree.com/assessment** or page 128 for a blank reproducible form of this figure.

Before you begin reading about and working with the first of the five phases in chapter 1, consider the Assessment Beliefs Survey (figure I.3) to begin dialogue that focuses on meaningful and engaging assessment practices.

To introduce and explore changing the culture of assessment, rate your agreement on the following five statements and then debate among colleagues the merits of the ideas and accompanying practices that would suggest your agreement or disagreement.

Assessment practices motivate students.

| Strongly Agree | Agree | Disagree | Strongly Disagree |

Assessments communicate learning.

| Strongly Agree | Agree | Disagree | Strongly Disagree |

Assessments reflect student strengths.

| Strongly Agree | Agree | Disagree | Strongly Disagree |

Assessments reveal a student's next steps in learning.

| Strongly Agree | Agree | Disagree | Strongly Disagree |

Mistakes and failure are embraced as opportunities to grow and learn.

| Strongly Agree | Agree | Disagree | Strongly Disagree |

Figure I.3: Assessment beliefs survey.

Visit **go.solution-tree.com/assessment** or page 136 for a blank reproducible form of this figure.

Next, fill out the Assessment Practices Strengths and Next-Steps Reflection (figure I.4, page 14). The reflection is designed to determine current levels of understanding and implementation of high-quality assessment practices. Individual teachers, teams, or administrators may use this assessment to identify strength and growth areas.

Individual teachers, teams, or schools may use this reflection to focus on certain aspects of this book as well as what professional learning would be most beneficial to move assessment practices forward and produce meaningful and engaging work for students. Visit **go.solution-tree.com/assessment** to download these tools.

Consider the following:

- What structures do you notice in these examples? How do they reflect the three design qualities? In what ways do they depart from the design qualities? How would you improve their design and use?

Use the following confidence-rating images to score the statements in the table.

★   I know what this is and do it regularly with intention.

✓   I know what this is but haven't done much of it yet.

?   I have questions about what this is and what it means.

Descriptive Statements of Assessment Practices	Confidence Rating	Next Steps
Clearly defined learning goals drive instruction.		
Clearly defined learning goals drive activities.		
Clearly defined learning goals drive assessments.		
Clearly defined learning goals drive grades or reporting practices.		
Assessment practices are balanced. Formative and summative practices are aligned and used intentionally.		
Students receive descriptive feedback that tells them what they know and what they need to do next.		
Students are invested in their learning (act on comments, use the information from their assessments to make revisions, analyze their mistakes, and set goals for their next steps in their learning).		
Assessments are designed well (that is, are accurate, free from bias, contain clear directions, and are valid and reliable).		
Assessment data (common or individual) are analyzed to determine individual students' learning strengths and needs.		
Assessment data (common or individual) are used to plan instructional responses at the classroom or team levels (assessment data drive instruction; students are working on concepts based on what the data say).		
Assessment data inform teachers' instruction, curriculum, and assessment.		

Figure I.4: Assessment practices strengths and next-steps reflection.

Visit **go.solution-tree.com/assessment** or page 137 for a blank reproducible form of this figure.

- What structures seem to contribute to meaningful and engaging assessment design?
- Consider "Review Your Current Assessment With the Three Design Qualities" (page 134). How could you use this protocol or form to improve assessments or dialogue about assessments you currently use?

Choosing Standards and Planning Engagement

When I design buildings, I think of the overall composition, much as the parts of a body would fit together. On top of that, I think about how people will approach the building and experience that space.

—Tadao Ando

In the same way an architect designs buildings, in designing a high-quality assessment, one has to consider both the overall composition, what we want students to do and show, as well as how students will approach and experience the assessment. Phase one in the Design in Five process consists of making decisions about the overall composition or scope of the assessment. Choosing the standards that will be assessed is the first step. It is also where we start to consider why these standards are important and what is intriguing, unique, essential, and relevant about focusing on them. This second step is where we plan engagement. What is interesting or unique about these standards? What possible topics, questions, or methods might capture students' interest (taking on the role of a scientist, writing a letter to an author, creating a solution to a problem occurring in the community).

Phase one of the Design in Five process consists of two steps.

1. Choose the standards.
2. Plan engagement.

Choose the Standards

Choose standards for the assessment you intend to create or revise during a targeted unit, segment of time, or theme. The task of choosing standards is informed by your national, state, and local context. However, teachers must decide when and how these standards are going to be taught and assessed at the classroom level. They are in the best position to understand their students' learning strengths, needs, interests, and motives and to make this learning relevant and meaningful. Some teachers organize learning by units, others by segments of time or theme. Many schools, districts, states, provinces, and national organizations have created documents to help guide the implementation of standards in instruction and assessment. Curriculum maps and pacing guides offer useful tools to help focus the creation or revision of assessments and, in particular, the first step of this phase, choosing standards. These are important documents to consult. When choosing standards, there are several important considerations.

What Is the Overall Purpose of This Assessment?

If creating a semester or final assessment, choose the most essential standards taught and intended for students to learn during the semester. These essential standards are critical for success in the next course and important to know beyond the assessment or test, as they prepare students for success in the future. A semester assessment, or final course assessment, does not need to be cumulative. In fact, at its best, it represents the engaging work at the deepest level required in that course.

When crafting an end-of-unit or theme assessment, target the standards intended to be mastered. Some teachers may craft an assessment for standards that recur and are addressed throughout a course or grade. This is often the case with standards in the early elementary years, as well as with writing, dialogue, mathematical standards of practice, and technical and literary reading. Teachers plan the timing and frequency of formative and summative assessments of the chosen standard during phase three.

When crafting a formative assessment, the chosen standard should be something absolutely essential for students to know and something that is perhaps hard to teach and hard to learn. Often the formative assessment is designed after the summative is designed. Teachers can reflect on the learning goals students need to achieve on the summative assessment and what learning goals might require more practice. Those learning goals become the target of any formative assessment.

Which Standards Are Emphasized in the Targeted Unit or Time Frame?

Given the local, state, or provincial context, what documents (curriculum maps, pacing guides, unit plans, and so on) inform the standards in the unit or time frame chosen for this assessment? Use these guidelines, if appropriate, to choose standards. They have often been placed with intention to ensure that alignment exists among grade levels and courses and that the most essential standards get the most amount of time in instruction and assessment.

What Cross-Disciplinary Critical Standards or Topics Are Relevant to This Assessment?

In many cases, an assessment targets multiple standards. This can work beautifully but also needs to be carefully planned so that students get ample practice and instruction to engage in the assessment effectively. For example, if students are writing to show their understanding or synthesis of multiple texts, there will be reading standards as well as writing standards chosen.

A ninth-grade teacher chose the following standards to shape the instruction and assessment of an English 9 unit focused on the American dream. Both include Reading and Speaking and Listening standards (NGA & CCSSO, 2010a).

- **RL.9–10.2:** Determine a theme or central idea of a text and analyze in detail its development over the course of the text, including how it emerges and is shaped and refined by specific details; provide an objective summary of the text. (p. 38)

- **SL.9–10.1:** Initiate and participate effectively in a range of collaborative discussions (one-on-one, in groups, and teacher-led) with diverse partners on *grades 9–10 topics, texts, and issues,* building on others' ideas and expressing their own clearly and persuasively. (p. 50)

- **SL.9–10.1a:** Come to discussions prepared, having read and researched material under study; explicitly draw on that preparation by referring to evidence from texts and other research on the topic or issue to stimulate a thoughtful, well-reasoned exchange of ideas. (p. 50)

- **SL.9–10.1b:** Work with peers to set rules for collegial discussions and decision-making (e.g., informal consensus, taking votes on key issues, presentation of alternate views), clear goals and deadlines, and individual roles as needed. (p. 50)

- **SL.9–10.1c:** Propel conversations by posing and responding to questions that relate the current discussion to broader themes or larger ideas; actively incorporate others into the discussion; and clarify, verify, or challenge ideas and conclusions. (p. 50)

- **SL.9–10.1d:** Respond thoughtfully to diverse perspectives, summarize points of agreement and disagreement, and, when warranted, qualify or justify their own views and understanding and make new connections in light of the evidence and reasoning presented. (p. 50)

Some standards will cycle throughout multiple units or themes or develop over time. And some standards may naturally cross disciplines or support other critical areas, such as writing and dialogue. Using evidence from the text to contribute to a dialogue can occur in social studies, science, literature, and business, among other areas. Writing to inform is a standard that can also apply to multiple disciplines. In math, students could use the concept of fractions to describe how they made a decision about how much pizza to buy for their class party. In chemistry, students might use what they know about tessellations to analyze a chemical reaction and inform others about their findings.

Consider standards that naturally cross disciplines or support other critical areas.

Let's look at another example, this time from a second-grade math team. They chose the following standard to ground a unit on money in the Common Core Measurement and Data domain.

> **2.MD.8:** Solve word problems involving dollar bills, quarters, dimes, nickels, and pennies, using $ and ¢ symbols appropriately. *Example: If you have 2 dimes and 3 pennies, how many cents do you have?* (NGA & CCSSO, 2010b, p. 20)

In addition to this standard, this team chose two Standards for Mathematical Practice on which to focus in this unit, as described in the Common Core (NGA & CCSSO, 2010b, pp. 6–7). They could have focused on other standards of practice as well, but chose this focus for this unit.

- **Mathematical Practice 3:** Construct viable arguments and critique the reasoning of others.

- **Mathematical Practice 4:** Model with mathematics.

Not only will students solve word problems using money, according to the standards, they will also explain their reasoning, critique others' solutions, and represent the solutions with a model (most likely, in this case, an equation).

While this first step seems rather simple, it is sometimes not as natural. In some cases, teachers start with a current assessment and look at it in general to determine if it loosely reflects the topic or essence of the standard. Textbook companies will also describe their assessments as aligned to standards. Whether teachers have assessments they are modifying, using textbook assessments, or creating them from scratch, choosing standards is an important first step. Looking at available documents that describe the scope and sequence of a course or grade level informs these choices. But, no matter what is available, looking through the standards and determining the focus of the assessment you will design is important, as it provides the foundation and the lens through which to design and critique the kinds of assessment items and tasks in which students engage.

Plan Engagement

The second step, planning engagement, is where we start to consider how students will *experience* the unit and standards and where they will find meaning. Phil Schlechty (2011) tells us that, "engaged students are attentive, persistent, and committed. They find value and meaning in the work and learn what they are expected to learn" (p. 14). Engaging and meaningful assessments offer students challenging work that sets them up for success throughout school and beyond.

Planning engagement, in effect, is planning for a meaningful response to the protest "Why do we have to know this?" Even though a reading assignment may be linked to an assessment, students need to know that the purpose and importance of the reading involve learning, enjoying, and acquiring information to evaluate a decision, and so on, not just to do well on a reading test. Intentionally planning and thinking about the meaning of the assessment is incredibly engaging for students. High school senior Gertrude Mongare (2009) reflects in an essay on the actions and words of teachers who had influenced her learning. Teachers are most effective, she writes, "if their students are able to learn something that they can carry . . . for the rest of their lives" rather than learning "information that they can't use because they do not know how to" (p. 5). Francis Harris (2009), another senior reflecting on powerful teaching practices, writes, "Science classes in general are very difficult for me. I enjoy them, but sometimes I think that my brain just doesn't work that way. One thing that helped in Mrs. P's class was that she made mostly everything relate to the real world somehow . . . it just helped me realize that there was a reason we need to know these things; it isn't just for the heck of it" (p. 4). Engagement is about creating connections for students.

Fostering Engagement

What does an engaging assessment look like? Sometimes it is a test that contains more complex tasks that ask students to apply what they know to an authentic situation or task. Sometimes it is a weblog or paper designed for an audience beyond just the teacher. Sometimes it is a presentation, dialogue, interview, or quiz that asks students to use what they are learning to solve problems, communicate ideas, or answer interesting questions. For example, third-grade students studying the water cycle might explain their understanding to a city water official and then ask the official a few questions, requesting a response. Or students learning about the Civil War might be asked to list its causes but also to write about the lasting influence of the war on contemporary U.S. society and politics.

> *What does an engaging assessment look like? Sometimes it is a test that asks students to apply what they know to an authentic situation or task.*

Potential Authentic Situations or Roles

When planning engagement, spend a little time brainstorming possible authentic connections. This isn't the time to actually craft the task, but it is the time to consider the options that might make this assessment relevant for students. For example, Myron Schwartz (2011), a chemistry and physics teacher at South Adams High School in Berne, Indiana, responds to student interest in learning to create a process for getting clean water to Haiti.

> "Lots and lots of dots, in blue water" is how a seven-year-old described the drowning victims to her mother. When consecutive hurricanes struck Haiti in 2009, a small village school lost over thirty schoolchildren, and the subsequent contamination of its wells produced a serious shortage of drinking water. In hearing of the account, my high school science students suggested: since we do all sorts of science labs, why can't we learn the same information by developing a way for them to purify their water?

Thus began the "dots in blue water" project. The efforts of these students—with the help of several engineers, chemists, and experts in water purification—resulted in a prototype that can filter and purify over fifty gallons of contaminated water to drinkability in a minute. Their critical thinking and problem solving contributed to the global community in amazing ways.

One way to consider engagement is to ask students to consider how their learning connects to or informs local and global problems. This kind of work requires students and teachers to reflect, ponder, wonder, struggle, and create. Given the complexity of the world in which we live and the world that our students will be living in and contributing to, it is nearly impossible that the solutions to our biggest problems will come from choice A, B, C, or D. James Bellanca, Robin Fogarty, and Brian Pete (2012) describe critical thinking as "the brick and mortar of problem solving and decision making" (p. 13). Problem solving involves both analyzing and evaluating in order to come to a solution. Clean problem solving usually follows some sort of algorithm that leads to one right answer, whereas messy problem solving involves authentic, complex problems that are challenging and have more than one solution, like the water purification challenge that Schwartz's students took up. It is in the messy problem-solving process that we tap into the creative process and find multiple solutions to authentic world issues (Bellanca et al., 2012).

Messy problem solving involves authentic, complex problems that are challenging and have more than one solution. It is in the messy problem-solving process that we tap into the creative process.

Potential Essential Questions

Essential questions that create interest and intrigue can be an important aspect of engagement. Considering these types of questions in the first phase helps open up the possibilities for the type of situations and tasks teachers design for the assessment (phases three and four). Jay McTighe and Grant Wiggins (2013) describe them as

> not answerable with finality in a single lesson or a brief sentence—and that's the point. Their aim is to stimulate thought, to provoke inquiry, and to spark more questions, including thoughtful student questions, not just pat answers. They are provocative and generative. By tackling such questions, learners are engaged in uncovering the depth and richness of a topic that might otherwise be obscured by simply covering it. (p. 3)

Student Interests and Ideas

Another piece of information that can influence the engaging aspect of the assessment design is asking students about their interests and ideas. It can be about what they enjoy doing, like athletics, games, music, and theater. For example, in geometry, students might analyze the best angles to use to shoot goals. It can also be about the issues and situations they are passionate about, like Schwartz's students' interest in developing a system to purify water. Figuring out what interests students by knowing what they feel passionate about and how they might be able to contribute to the school, local, or global community provides many engaging possibilities.

Authentic situations, meaningful roles, essential questions, and student interests are all possible ways to create engagement. (In phase one, planning engagement is about generating potential ideas and does not include all of these things.) In any given assessment there will be a better choice that is based on effectiveness and efficiency. Generating an essential question or having students take on a role is much less intense then generating a solution to a global problem and actually making it happen. There is a time and a place for both at all grade levels and in all courses.

Using Questions to Guide Engagement Planning

Use the following questions to guide your engagement planning.

- What key ideas do you want to last beyond the unit?

- What themes give this unit relevance and coherence?

- What is the *why* of the unit?

- What ideas and questions create a sense of intrigue?

- How do experts or masters of this discipline use the information?

- What processes are used to solve problems and learn concepts?

- What stories, experiences, symbols, and traditions from your students' cultural backgrounds could influence the way you formulate essential questions, authentic roles or scenarios, and assessments?

In the ninth-grade unit focused on the American dream, a teacher framed student learning around an essential question to generate engagement and set up the summative assessment (to be developed in phases three and four). How has the American dream changed over time? Many texts describe the American experience across decades: "I Hear America Singing" by Walt Whitman (1860), "Winter Dreams" by F. Scott Fitzgerald (1926), "Dreaming America" by Joyce Carol Oates (1973), and so on. See Center for the Study of the American Dream (2014) for a survey on the American dream and Linn (2013) for a news story questioning the state of the American dream. The goal is to frame the learning around an engaging idea and incorporate resources and ideas that students can experience and explore.

The engaging idea that grounds the second-grade unit on money is: "Knowing the value of money and how to add and subtract money helps me make smart choices about how to spend and save." Students need to know how to add money to purchase a candy bar, and they need to know that if they buy the candy bar, they may not have enough money left for the coloring book. This encompasses not only solving problems but also communicating, collaborating, reasoning, and modeling—all of which relate to the standards this second-grade team wants students to learn and experience during this unit. In this example, teachers noticed how interested students were in making money to buy things they really wanted. Tying money to this interest was a small but significant step in helping students see relevance in the work they were doing.

Putting Phase One Into Play

When putting phase one into play, document the standards and the engaging ideas that inform the assessment design and instruction. When identifying an engaging idea, it may be one such as the essential question for the American dream unit or the statement for the second-grade math unit. But it could also be a list of possible topics, questions, scenarios, or roles to be developed as the assessment unfolds. Note when some standards recur over the course of the year through multiple units; by identifying those spiraling standards, you will be able to use rubrics or scoring guides you have created again later. Also, when beginning this process of documenting in phase one, choose just one assessment for one unit or time frame. It can be too overwhelming to think about and plan every assessment right away. The process will move faster as you implement it more often. (Visit **go.solution-tree.com/assessment** to listen to a screencast of Nicole modeling phases one and two for a fifth-grade reading assessment).

Figures 1.1 and 1.2 (page 22) show how phase one would be documented for the ninth-grade American dream unit and the second-grade unit on money, respectively.

Grade Level and Focus
Ninth-Grade American Dream Unit
Engagement Ideas
How has the American dream changed over time?
Standards
• **RL.9–10.2:** Determine a theme or central idea of a text and analyze in detail its development over the course of the text, including how it emerges and is shaped and refined by specific details; provide an objective summary of the text. • **SL.9–10.1:** Initiate and participate effectively in a range of collaborative discussions (one-on-one, in groups, and teacher-led) with diverse partners on grades 9–10 topics, texts, and issues, building on others' ideas and expressing their own clearly and persuasively. • **SL.9–10.1a:** Come to discussions prepared, having read and researched material under study; explicitly draw on that preparation by referring to evidence from texts and other research on the topic or issue to stimulate a thoughtful, well-reasoned exchange of ideas. • **SL.9–10.1b:** Work with peers to set rules for collegial discussions and decision-making (e.g., informal consensus, taking votes on key issues, presentation of alternate views), clear goals and deadlines, and individual roles as needed. • **SL.9–10.1c:** Propel conversations by posing and responding to questions that relate the current discussion to broader themes or larger ideas; actively incorporate others into the discussion; and clarify, verify, or challenge ideas and conclusions. • **SL.9–10.1d:** Respond thoughtfully to diverse perspectives, summarize points of agreement and disagreement, and when warranted, qualify or justify their own views and understanding and make new connections in light of the evidence and reasoning presented. • **CCRA.R.9:** Analyze how two or more texts address similar themes or topics in order to build knowledge or to compare the approaches the authors take.

Source: NGA & CCSSO, 2010a, p. 10, 38, 50.

Figure 1.1: Engagement plan and standards for the ninth-grade American dream unit.

Grade Level and Focus
Second-Grade Unit on Money
Engagement Ideas
Knowing the value of money and how to add and subtract money helps me make smart choices about how to spend and save.
Standards
• **2.MD.8:** Solve word problems involving dollar bills, quarters, dimes, nickels, and pennies, using $ and ¢ symbols appropriately. *Example: If you have 2 dimes and 3 pennies, how many cents do you have?* • **Mathematical Practice 3:** Construct viable arguments and critique the reasoning of others. • **Mathematical Practice 4:** Model with mathematics.
Note
Students will focus on solving word problems using money and explain their reasoning, critique others' solutions, and represent the solution with a model (most likely with an equation).

Source: NGA & CCSSO, 2010b, pp. 6–7, 20.

Figure 1.2: Engagement plan and standards for the second-grade unit on money.

Visit **go.solution-tree.com/assessment** or page 139 for a blank reproducible form of this figure.

Pause and Ponder

The following questions are designed to help individual teachers or teams focus on the essential ideas presented in this chapter.

- Knowing that essential questions, engaging scenarios, and roles are not new concepts, talk about your understanding of how they contribute to meaning and engagement in an assessment.

- Make connections to current and past work. How do these ideas connect to what you are currently doing or to work you have done in the past?

- What kind of information do you currently gather about student interests and passions? What kinds of local and global connections are available and possible given your context?

- What do you already have in place? What key ideas from this chapter are important for taking your assessments to the next level?

- Note what questions emerge as you listen to the screencast describing phase one (at **go.solution-tree.com/assessment**).

- Choose a unit or a time frame. Individually, or with your team, identify the standards and plan engagement for this unit and then debrief.

  - What worked about the process? What went smoothly?

  - What was most challenging?

  - What tips or tricks might you consider using when you do this phase again?

Analyzing the Standards and Sketching Out Learning Goals

One of the most powerful things you can do for the people around you is provide clarity. Clarity empowers people, improves execution, and allows for greater accountability. I always try to keep in mind the quote by Lewis Carroll—"If you don't know where you are going, any road will get you there."

—Tom Carroll

Clarity is the key word for phase two of the Design in Five process. Through analyzing the standards and sketching out the learning goals for the unit or time frame, teachers make meaning of and gain clarity about the learning they want for their students. Learning goals are the foundation for designing an engaging assessment that provides meaningful information about a student's understanding and achievement.

There are two steps within this phase.

1. Analyze the standards.
2. Sketch out the learning goals.

Analyze the Standards

A second-grade team was reviewing the results of a recent assessment on poetry. The students had scored well, and the team members were discussing their next steps in helping the students grow. The focus of the assessment was on identifying rhythm and rhyme in poems. When looking back at the standard, however, they realized the assessment had missed the mark.

RL.2.4: Describe how words and phrases (e.g., regular beats, alliteration, rhymes, repeated lines) supply rhythm and meaning in a story, poem, or song. (NGA & CCSSO, 2010a, p. 11)

The standard clearly articulates that students need to describe how words are used to create meaning, which is different than identifying the rhyme pattern or number of syllables in a line. Nothing in the assessment gave the teachers any information about how students could describe the way poets use rhythm and rhyme to create meaning. Nicole worked with the team to write a new assessment that asked students to read a couple of poems and address why words repeated and how the meaning might change with different words. They included questions about rhyme patterns and rhythm in terms of syllables, but overall the questions emphasized how rhythm and rhyme influenced the meaning of the poem. Figure 2.1 contains an excerpt of the assessment.

Name: _____ Date: _____

Targets

I can find rhyme and rhythm in a story, poem, or song.

I can describe how words and phrases supply rhythm and meaning in a story, poem, or song.

"Who Has Seen the Wind?" by Christina Rossetti (1947)

Write the number of syllables
in each line in the space provided.

Who has seen the wind?   _____

Neither I nor you: _____

But when the leaves hang trembling,   _____

The wind is passing through.   _____

Who has seen the wind?   _____

Neither you nor I: _____

But when the trees bow down their heads, _____

The wind is passing by.   _____

1. Circle the rhyming words in the first stanza.

2. Circle the rhyming words in the second stanza.

3. Count the syllables in each line and write the number on the line provided.

4. What words or phrases does the poet repeat?

5. Why do you think the poet repeats these words or phrases? Explain how it contributed to the meaning of the poem.

_____

_____

_____

_____

_____

6. Your teacher will read another version of the poem. What sounds different? How does it change?

_____

_____

_____

_____

_____

7. Does this change make the poem better? Why or why not?

_____

_____

_____

_____

_____

Figure 2.1: Assessing rhythm, rhyme, and meaning in poetry.

Visit **go.solution-tree.com/assessment** for a reproducible version of this assessment.

Analyzing the standards is about individuals and teams of teachers making sense of and interpreting the standards in order to plan instruction and assessment that reflects this interpretation. While there are documents and resources, such as curriculum guides, that describe standards and break them down into learning goals for teachers (and such documents are worth having at the table when designing assessments), the actual process used to understand and make meaning of the standards must be taken up by individuals and teams. For example, a kindergarten team had access to all of their standards and accompanying learning goals through a webpage their district developed. This was a fantastic resource, but the team still needed to look at the standards, determine a focus for the assessment they were designing, and talk about the meaning of the learning goals in terms of what students would actually do.

In some cases, the standard articulates the bottom-line expectation. When this is this case, teachers agree to a minimum standard but also describe the more complex levels that are necessary for engagement and growth.

To engage in this phase of Design in Five, obtain a copy of the standards identified in phase one and any accompanying documents. Then, individually or with your team, do the following.

1. **Circle the verbs (and other words that indicate what students should do) in the standards:** Why verbs? These words lead us to the cognitive level required and the type of work in which our students need to engage. For example, the phrase *identify literary elements* means something different than *analyze and use evidence to support the use of literary elements*. Asking a student to identify *irony*, which could be assessed by a multiple-choice item, is different from asking a student to explain why an author chose to employ irony, which would require engagement with the text and a verbal or written description produced by the student.

2. **Underline key concepts, vocabulary words, and contextual information:** It is helpful to consider the concepts and topics used in the standards. A focus on vocabulary is essential for all students but is especially important for English learners, as they navigate not only the concepts but also another language. Consideration of concepts and vocabulary also helps inform instruction and the type of academic language pertinent to the grade level and content area. In some cases, students are asked to consider the same concept or topic from multiple perspectives. This means students have to read about the same event or the same concept and pay attention to context and to where the message is coming from. In another example, students might need to study a concept using multiple resources—not just written text, but audio and video as well. Underlining the key words, concepts, and contexts in the standards will help inform assessment design.

An example of the analyzing step of phase two is found in figure 2.2. You can also visit **go.solution-tree .com/assessment** to find more examples.

7. Integrate quantitative or technical information expressed in words in a text with a version of that information expressed visually (for example, in a flowchart, diagram, model, graph, or table).

8. Distinguish among facts, reasoned judgment based on research findings, and speculation in a text.

9. Compare and contrast the information gained from experiments, simulations, video, or multimedia sources with that gained from reading a text on the same topic.

Figure 2.2: Circling verbs and underlining key concepts for reading standards.

When standards are new or unfamiliar, consider doing the following on a first read.

- Star what is familiar—which standards have they already taught and assessed?
- Place question marks and notes by standards that are confusing or that need clarification.
- Circle standards or language not yet taught or assessed.

At times it is also helpful to look at how the standards align vertically. What are students expected to do right before and right after the targeted standard? For example, if you are focused on a fourth-grade assessment on fractions, look at the third-grade standards on fractions, if any, as well as the fifth-grade standards on fractions and consider the following.

- What would the student work look like at each level?
- How does the task or cognitive level change among grade levels?
- How is the cognitive level similar among grade levels?
- How do these differences inform the assessment design?
- What is one thing I might do to prepare students for the next grade level or course?

After doing focus groups with sixth, seventh, eighth, and ninth graders in one school district, it became clear that students did the same poetry project and the same health project in both middle and high school. Reviewing vertical alignment can save time in our instruction and assessment.

Sketch Out the Learning Goals

Learning goals are statements describing what students should know and be able to do—the knowledge and skills required for students to achieve a standard. Learning goals tightly align to the standards, representing the learning students need to reflect the essence of the standards. Some educators frame learning goals as "I can" statements, a strategy recommended by Rick Stiggins, Judith Arter, Jan Chappuis, and Stephen Chappuis (2004), to make them student friendly. Teasing out the learning goals from standards creates the foundation for our instruction (lesson plans, activities), our assessments (both formative and summative), and our curriculum (the resources tapped to plan instruction and assessment).

To construct a learning goal, start with the standard you have analyzed. The intention is to write learning goals that represent the standard. Each learning goal identifies one part of what students need to achieve to master the standard. Use the action words you have circled, or substitute a more descriptive action that describes what you want students to know or be able to do. Then explain it.

The number of learning goals written for any given standard will vary based on how complex the standard is and how many parts it contains, but making the learning goals reflect the parts needed to achieve the standard is the goal. The learning goals will eventually be what teachers target in the assessment. Sometimes prerequisite learning goals are needed. These are not directly in the standard but will need to be addressed for students to achieve it. For example, in the sixth- to eighth-grade Reading standard in figure 2.2, a prerequisite learning goal might be, "I can describe visual representations of quantitative information." In addition, when considering how to push students in applying these concepts at deeper levels, consider how these concepts are used in authentic situations. In this case, I would add another learning goal, "I can use quantitative, technical information and visually displayed information to pose solutions to authentic situations." This communicates how this standard is relevant and in what context this learning might be applied.

Translating these analyzed standards into learning goals with a friendlier "I can" frame might yield the following.

1. I can integrate quantitative or technical information with a visual of that information.

2. I can distinguish between and among facts, reasoned judgments, and speculation in a text.

3. I can compare and contrast information from experiments, simulations, video, or other multimedia sources with that in a text on the same topic.

The potential prerequisite learning goals are as follows.

1. I can summarize information made in research reports, videos, and other texts.

2. I can identify speculation in texts.

3. I can describe visual representations of quantitative information.

A potentially deeper learning goal is: I can use quantitative, technical information and visually displayed information to pose solutions to authentic situations.

In this case, there were three learning goals that reflected each part of the standard. There could be a fourth if I had separated the last one into "I can compare . . . " and another that read "I can contrast information from experiments, simulations, video, or other multimedia sources with that in a text on the same topic." It is not necessary to do this, but I will need to pay close attention to the items I design to ensure they ask students to both compare and contrast. These *learning goals* represent what students need to achieve in order to master the standard.

Consider the context for these learning goals as well. In what situations or contexts must students demonstrate them? In the sixth- through eighth-grade example, "reading a text on the same topic" is underlined to indicate that students need to compare and contrast simulations or videos with another text they have read dealing with the same topic. That influences the resources and materials teachers need to gather for the assessment and the tasks they will create. For example, students may be asked to analyze and synthesize multiple texts versus one text. In addition, is there language in the standard that asks students to write, analyze, or create? Students might write up the statements from their science investigation for an authentic audience—crafting a one-page brochure geared to help elementary students consider the best food to feed a plant if you want to keep it alive. But, we're getting ahead of ourselves. At this point, we are only figuring out the meaning of our standards to create learning goals. However, if I want to incorporate writing into the assessment, it would be appropriate to include a writing standard as well. There is a fine line between considering the activities and assessment in general terms and planning what specific type of student work we want students to engage in. When determining if the verb is specific enough or if there is uncertainty about what standards to include, ask the question: "What would the student work look like that would represent student's achievement of this standard, or learning goal?" That can help guide the discussion to lead to a more specific verb and better understanding of the learning goal.

Once learning goals are identified, individual or teams of teachers determine their complexity and rigor. When considering complexity, select a framework or create your own for different levels of cognition. Bloom's taxonomy (Forehand, 2005), Webb's Depth of Knowledge (Hess, 2006), and Marzano and Kendall's (2007) taxonomy are among the most common frameworks readily available and most often used in assessment and instruction design. Following are verbs used for the Design in Five process in levels of complexity that can easily be adapted to your own framework.

- **Simple:** *Define, recognize, describe, explain, recall, identify, relate, label, review, memorize, state, name, summarize, compute*

- **Complex:** *Apply, analyze, connect, examine, appraise, categorize, distinguish, compare, infer, classify, interpret, contrast, predict, recommend, differentiate, support, defend, formulate, judge, evaluate, criticize, synthesize, investigate*

- **More complex verbs that involve doing:** *Operate, make, calculate, match, compose, measure, construct, plan, demonstrate, practice, show, use*

- **More complex verbs that involve creating:** *Produce, create, write, design, develop*

Use a learning goals ladder to put the learning goals in order of complexity. This process of "ordering" learning goals helps get a sense of how the parts (individual learning goals) are working together to help students understand and achieve standards. Teams have found this conversation helps deepen their understanding of the learning goals and what they really want students doing. The ladder shown in figure 2.3

I can use quantitative, technical information and visually displayed information to pose solutions to authentic situations.

I can integrate quantitative or technical information with a visual of that information.

I can compare and contrast information from experiments, simulations, video, or other multimedia sources with that in a text on the same topic.

I can summarize information made in research reports, videos, and other texts.

I can distinguish between and among facts, reasoned judgments, and speculation in a text.

I can describe visual representations of quantitative information.

I can identify speculation in texts.

Figure 2.3: A learning goals ladder.

Visit **go.solution-tree.com/assessment** or page 140 for a blank reproducible form of this figure.

is an example of the learning goals identified from figure 2.2, which outlines the sixth- to eighth-grade reading standards for technical literacy.

If the progression of complexity is not applicable, simply identify the criteria embedded in the standard. This often involves creating an outline of a rubric that can be used to assess whatever tasks are chosen to provide evidence of students' achievement.

Too often, we craft learning goals but don't move fast enough to tie those goals to specific student work in our assessment and instructional practice. In the absence of that crucial step, it often seems to teachers that they are recreating documents that already have been designed to describe the learning or curriculum. At the 2013 Minnetonka Institute for Leadership in Minnetonka, Minnesota, Grant Wiggins likens the standards to building codes needed to construct a safe and secure building. Beyond fulfilling the basic demands of the code are designers, architects, and others who build for a specific time, place, and purpose and for a targeted audience. This process of coming to know, understand, and integrate the standards through sketching out learning goals and then intentionally design engaging assessments is part of the art of teaching. Once we have deeper understanding of how these learning goals work together to help students achieve, we can move to phase three, where we start to describe the student work that will help teachers gather information about student achievement on these standards.

Put Phase Two Into Play

Visit **go.solution-tree.com/assessment** to listen to a screencast modeling phases one and two of a fifth-grade reading assessment. Following is an example of phase two in action, using the American dream unit.

The first step is to circle the action words and underline important phrases in the standards (figure 2.4, page 30).

Grade Level and Focus
Ninth-Grade American Dream Unit

Engaging Question, Statement, or Authentic Context
How has the American dream changed over time?

Standards

- **RL.9–10.2:** Determine a theme or central idea of a text and analyze in detail its development over the course of the text, including how it emerges and is shaped and refined by specific details; provide an objective summary of the text.

- **SL.9–10.1:** Initiate and participate effectively in a range of collaborative discussions (one-on-one, in groups, and teacher-led) with diverse partners on grades 9–10 topics, texts, and issues, building on others' ideas and expressing their own clearly and persuasively.

- **SL.9–10.1a:** Come to discussions prepared, having read and researched material under study; explicitly draw on that preparation by referring to evidence from texts and other research on the topic or issue to stimulate a thoughtful, well-reasoned exchange of ideas.

- **SL.9–10.1b:** Work with peers to set rules for collegial discussions and decision-making (e.g., informal consensus, taking votes on key issues, presentation of alternate views), clear goals and deadlines, and individual roles as needed.

- **SL.9–10.1c:** Propel conversations by posing and responding to questions that relate the current discussion to broader themes or larger ideas; actively incorporate others into the discussion; and clarify, verify, or challenge ideas and conclusions.

- **SL.9–10.1d:** Respond thoughtfully to diverse perspectives, summarize points of agreement and disagreement, and, when warranted, qualify or justify their own views and understanding and make new connections in light of the evidence and reasoning presented.

- **CCRA.R.9:** Analyze how two or more texts address similar themes or topics in order to build knowledge or to compare the approaches the authors take.

Source: NGA & CCSSO, 2010a, p. 10, 38, 50.

Figure 2.4: Circling verbs and underlining key concepts for an ELA-literacy unit.

The next step is to create a list of learning goals in the form of "I can" statements generated from the circling and underlining.

- I can analyze the key messages in a text.

- I can compare and contrast key messages in multiple texts on the same topic.

- I can describe the approaches authors make in their texts.

- I can produce an objective summary of a text.

- I can determine the central idea or theme in a text.

- I can analyze the details that lead to the theme over the course of a text.

- I can describe how the theme emerges and is shaped.

- I can use evidence from the texts I have read to generate dialogue.

- I can respond to questions in a dialogue.

- I can summarize points of agreement and disagreement.

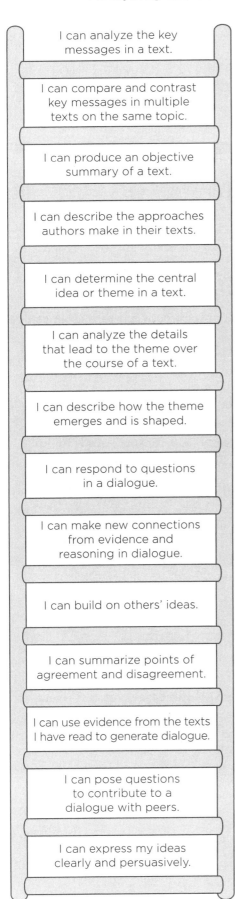

Figure 2.5: Learning ladder for American dream unit.

- I can make new connections from evidence and reasoning in dialogue.

- I can build on others' ideas.

- I can pose questions to contribute to a dialogue with peers.

- I can express my ideas clearly and persuasively.

Once you have made a list, create a learning ladder by listing the learning goals in order of complexity, as shown in figure 2.5.

Figures 2.6 and 2.7 (page 32) show how to put phase two into play for a second-grade unit on money. In figure 2.6, the important verbs are circled in the standards.

| **Grade Level and Focus** |
| Second-Grade Unit on Money |

| **Engaging Question, Statement, or Authentic Context** |
| Knowing the value of money and how to add and subtract money helps me make smart choices about how to spend and save. |

Standards

- **2.MD.8:** Solve word problems involving dollar bills, quarters, dimes, nickels, and pennies, using $ and ¢ symbols appropriately. *Example: If you have 2 dimes and 3 pennies, how many cents do you have?*

- **Mathematical Practice 3:** Construct viable arguments and critique the reasoning of others.

- **Mathematical Practice 4:** Model with mathematics.

NOTE: Students will focus on students solving word problems using money, and also explaining their reasoning, critiquing others' solutions, and representing the solution with a model (most likely with an equation).

Source: NGA & CCSSO, 2010b, pp. 6–7, 20.

Figure 2.6: Circling action words and underlining key concepts for a measurement and data unit.

The next step is to create a list of learning goals in the form of "I can" statements generated from the circling and underlining.

- I can critique another mathematician's solution.
- I can make a model for my solution.
- I can use what I know about coins to solve real-world problems.
- I can add money.
- I can identify coins and their values.
- I can construct an argument supporting the process I used to solve the problem.

Finally, create a learning ladder by listing the learning goals in order of complexity, as shown in figure 2.7.

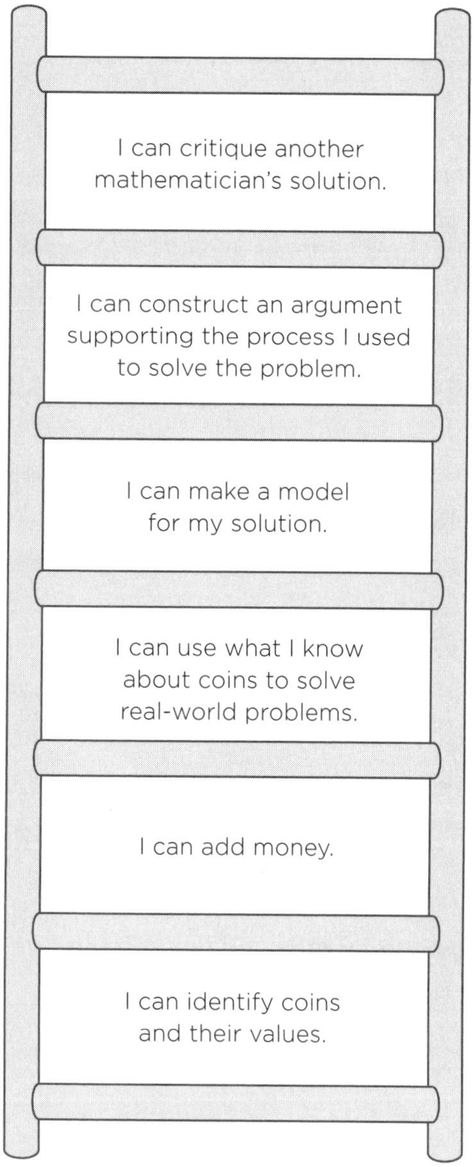

Pause and Ponder

The following questions are designed to help individual teachers or teams focus on the essential ideas presented in this chapter.

- Describe what it means to analyze the standards. What is the purpose of analyzing standards? What are the benefits and challenges of this process? What, if any, has been your experience with this process in the past? What purpose has it served?

- Describe learning goals. What are they, and what purpose do they serve? What do you call or have you called learning goals: objectives, expectations, or something else? Language is really important, and making connections to your past work can make this process more effective and focused.

- Just for fun (yes, you may question my idea of fun), put the following learning goals in order from simple to complex. After you have done that, consider what occurred in your thinking or dialogue while trying to make these decisions. After you have finished, visit **go.solution-tree.com/assessment** to take a look at one team's version of this. Please note, this is not the *right* answer; it's just one way a group of teachers made sense of this.

Ladder (top to bottom):
- I can critique another mathematician's solution.
- I can construct an argument supporting the process I used to solve the problem.
- I can make a model for my solution.
- I can use what I know about coins to solve real-world problems.
- I can add money.
- I can identify coins and their values.

Figure 2.7: Learning ladder for second-grade money unit.

- I can describe characters and setting.
- I can explain how characters in the story respond to challenges.
- I can summarize text.
- I can quote accurately from the text.
- I can determine the theme or central idea from details in the text.

- How does thinking about the way learning goals work together or work cognitively benefit assessment and instruction?
- Continue to try out the process by analyzing standards and writing and organizing learning goals for the standards identified at the end of chapter 1. Then talk about what worked and what was challenging about the process.

Crafting an Assessment Plan

A good plan is like a road map: it shows the final destination and usually the best way to get there.

—H. Stanley Judd

A team of social studies teachers crafted what they thought was a high-quality assessment during a summer work session. After a review of the assessment, where they identified the learning goal and complexity level of each item, they realized the assessment reflected neither the cognitive level of the standards nor what they expected their students to achieve. Phase three is designed to plan the design of assessment items and tasks so the assessment matches tightly to the learning goals and the rigor of the standard. This is the beginning of creating classroom assessments that are valid and reliable.

Validity and reliability are two important factors to consider when planning the assessment. Validity is useful for gaining quality information that provides good inferences about student learning. Construct validity is an aspect of validity that asks questions about the extent to which any task or item provides information about the targeted construct, in our case learning goals, and is sometimes referred to as content validity. The validation is strongest when a particular score or description of proficiency is supported by solid evidence. Validity involves the likelihood that those inferences are accurate and a useful interpretation of student learning (Bonner, 2013). The more reasons that students do poorly or do not demonstrate achievement of the intended learning goal, the lower the validity of the assessment or the weaker the inference. Also, the more reasons that students do well on an assessment that are unrelated to what the assessment was intended to demonstrate or estimate, the lower the validity of the assessment. For example, if the room is hot and the vocabulary is misaligned to instruction, students might miss questions—not because they don't understand the concept but because the vocabulary was unfamiliar and the room too hot.

Sarah M. Bonner (2013) discusses the practice of creating a test blueprint to increase classroom assessment validity, citing Tom Guskey's (2005) piece that describes the power of this type of planning. This assessment plan is grounded in that idea and empowers busy classroom teachers to engage in this type of planning on essential standards and assessments. Chapter 4 offers guidelines to create high-quality tasks and rubrics that empower teachers to create and revise assessments that provide solid inferences about learning.

Reliability is the second important characteristic of assessment design. Reliability "is the consistency with which any assessment provides a picture of proficiency or the degree of consistency between two measures of the same thing" (Lehmann & Mehrens, 1987, p. 38). Again, it is important for teachers to consider the evidence they are using to assign a grade or a mark. Is there enough evidence? Is it varied and available in multiple contexts and multiple ways? Jay Parkes (2013) identifies replication and sampling as two essential considerations for reliability: "Multiple items or tasks, multiple raters or judges, or multiple assessment times are required to assess the reliability of the scores" (p. 108). This informs the overall assessment plan. Teachers consider how many items to include in an individual test or task. Considerations are made for how often students will engage in a task. Finally, teachers can work with colleagues to score student work together on essential tasks. Reliability and validity depend on teachers being intentional about the type and frequency of student work used to make instructional decisions and report progress.

Once the simple and complex learning goals (phase two) have been established and it is clear how the parts (or individual learning goals) work together to create a picture of what students will achieve, craft an assessment plan that will connect the student work, or method of assessment, with the learning goals. This third phase has three steps.

1. Identify the learning goals for the assessment (chosen from the ladder created in phase two).

2. Choose the method of assessment.

3. Determine the weight and number of items for each learning goal.

Figure 3.1 illustrates a sample assessment plan based on the ninth-grade American dream unit.

Learning Goals	Method	Weight	Total Number of Points
I can use evidence from the texts I have read to generate dialogue.	Graphic, Educreations, or visual illustration showing the various perspectives. Socratic dialogue (rubric and student chart)	30 percent	25 points
I can summarize points of agreement and disagreement.			
I can compare and contrast key messages in multiple texts on the same topic.			
I can produce an objective summary of a text.	Essay and graphic organizer with accompanying scoring guide Socratic dialogue (rubric and student chart)	50 percent	40 points
I can determine the central idea or theme in a text.			
I can analyze the details that lead to the theme over the course of a text.			
I can describe how the theme emerges and is shaped.			
I can build on others' ideas.	Multiple-choice questions paired with short explanations	20 percent	Six questions per text for a total of 18 points

Figure 3.1: Assessment plan for American dream unit using the assessment plan template.

Visit **go.solution-tree.com/assessment** or page 141 for a blank reproducible form of this figure.

Identify the Learning Goals for the Assessment

The ladders of learning goals written in phase two inform (and in some cases *are*) the learning goals identified for the assessment plan. Some schools start designing formative assessments, while others begin with summative assessments. There are benefits and challenges to both approaches.

Starting with formative assessments means that teachers design checkpoints (both informal and formal) based on the learning goals of phase two. Teachers plan these assessments to ensure that students are well prepared to demonstrate their understanding summatively at the end of the unit or identified time frame.

When planning a formative assessment, teams or individuals identify one or just a few learning goals from the ladder. Following the formative assessment, teachers and students must take the time to respond to what they learn from the data. Thus, the best learning goals to choose are often those that students struggle with or need more time to learn. Teachers who have been doing this awhile know and can predict where students will struggle and choose essential-to-know, hard-to-teach, and hard-to-learn concepts.

The intent of a formative assessment is to provide results that a teacher can use to plan a lesson in which students fix their mistakes or revise their work. These check-ins may be in the form of quizzes, rough drafts of paragraphs, or a few real-world math problems, to name a few. In essence, formative assessment should be seen as lesson planning, not something added on top of a teacher's already full plate. Teachers analyze the student work and the data from these assessments and plan and modify instruction in ways that will help students understand or produce better work. Through formative assessments, students become more invested in their learning,

> *In a formative assessment, teachers select one or just a few learning goals that consist of essential-to-know, hard-to-teach, and hard-to-learn concepts.*

and getting the instruction they need inevitably helps them learn more and at higher levels (Hattie, 2009; McMillan, 2013; Wiliam, 2011). The challenge of doing formative assessments first is that there may be only a vague picture of what the end looks like and so, in some cases, what is assessed on the formative task may not give teachers and students enough information about what to practice or improve to be successful on the summative task. If students do well on the formative and not so well on the summative, this can indicate an alignment issue. For example, students may have demonstrated mastery in identifying the main idea on a short formative assessment. If they get to the summative task and have not practiced how to use evidence from the text to support that main idea, they may not do well, because it is the first time they have had to independently put all of the pieces (learning goals) together. This challenge can be addressed by starting with the design of a summative assessment. If an alignment issue emerges and it appears students do poorly on the summative because they have not practiced putting all pieces together, teachers can address this by giving students another opportunity to revise their work on the summative assessment.

Summative assessments are designed to determine a level of proficiency on the intended standards and learning goals at a moment in time, usually at the end of a unit or time frame. When planning a summative assessment—a unit test or a performance task such as a paper, weblog, Educreations whiteboard (www.educreations.com), or presentation—teachers look at the ladder of learning goals outlined in phase two. In many cases, all of those learning goals will be assessed on a summative assessment. Accurate information may require that the assessment have multiple parts. If so, this is determined in the planning. When considering a summative assessment for the end of a unit, choose the learning goals from those that are on the ladder. In the summative assessment plan for the ninth-grade American dream unit (figure 3.1, page 36), for example, the learning goals include all but a few that were on the ladder (page 31). In this particular unit, the eliminated learning goals were assessed summatively on another quiz earlier in the unit. There is no need to re-assess them unless students have not mastered them or they are essential. In other cases, the learning goals are prerequisites and need to be addressed in instruction, but it is not necessary to explicitly address them in a summative assessment where students are engaging in a task to show what they can do with what they have learned at the standard level.

When planning a summative assessment first, teachers gain a clear picture of what students need to do or create to show mastery of the intended standards and learning goals. When this end picture is clear, teachers more tightly align their instruction and formative assessments with that picture to ensure that students have ample time to practice independently to be able to successfully achieve the intended learning. Grant Wiggins and Jay McTighe (2005) talk about beginning with the end in mind in designing units and assessments. Starting with the design of a summative assessment is exactly that concept. Students also benefit from teachers having a clearer picture of the summative assessment or student work required to show proficiency. For students to benefit, teachers share with students the learning goals and the student work required to show an understanding of them. This creates a road map for students who, in turn, gain a clearer idea of how the learning goals they are working on (through instructional activities and formative assessments) are going to help them be successful on the summative assessment. When planned in this way, teaching to the test or task is not a limiting practice, because the learning is driving the assessment, as opposed to the test driving the learning. (If all test methods are reflective of one type of student work, they limit the ways in which students demonstrate their learning.) The challenge, again, is that in some cases, there may be a lack of alignment between formative and summative assessment. This can happen when a teacher doesn't get around to the formative assessment, because the planning was focused on the summative. Students may be faced with a summative assessment that asks them to apply learning that they may or may not have done before. This can easily be addressed through intentional instructional planning that focuses on the learning experiences needed to successfully demonstrate the standard on that summative assessment.

In either case, planning begins with choosing the learning goals for the assessment being created or revised.

Choose the Method of Assessment

Creating the ladder of learning goals (phase two) and the assessment plan (phase three) leads to clarity about the methods, or student work, that will yield information about where students are in their level of achievement. The next step in this phase is therefore to choose a method or type of assessment item and task that best reflects the intended learning (which corresponds to the second column of the assessment plan template; see figure 3.1, page 36).

When choosing a method, consider both effectiveness (it will ensure that students are doing the intended work at the cognitive level described) and efficiency (it is a realistic process for teacher and student in terms of time and score). The important question in planning the method is always, What is the type of student work that will reflect the learning goals or the achievement desired?

Identifying the verb in the learning goal is essential in finding the best method. If my learning goal (taken from the second-grade money unit ladder) is "I can construct an argument supporting the process I used to solve the problem," I cannot use a multiple-choice item because the verb *construct*, in my interpretation, means students are explaining the process they used to come to the solution. If my learning goal was "I can identify the best strategy to solve the problem," I could use a multiple-choice item that asks students to select the best strategy from among several choices. In this case, they are doing some evaluation as well. However, in order to understand fully if students had grasped the strategy, we would also have to ask them to explain their choice.

For another example of connecting the best method, or student work, to learning goals, refer to the American dream unit assessment plan (figure 3.1, page 36). When considering if students can identify key details in text, a multiple-choice method is both effective and efficient. However, for the next set of learning goals in the American dream unit—students need to describe the emerging theme, analyze the details that support this theme, determine the central idea, and produce an objective summary—students will need to create or produce something, and multiple choice will not work. For this set of learning goals, students will engage in a Socratic dialogue (and will be scored on their dialogue using a rubric) and create a graphic and an essay. In this example, I would also consider a formative assessment, because students will need to experience dialoging and writing an essay before being asked to use those methods on the summative assessment. In my instructional plans, I would be sure to use a Socratic dialogue a few times as a formative assessment, offer students feedback on their comments and questions, and give them another chance to practice dialogue with that feedback. If the best method to use is one that is unfamiliar to students, we have to carefully teach them how to use it. If not, they may do poorly—not because they have failed to achieve the learning goal but because they are unacquainted with the method. If the learning goal is "I can explain my problem-solving process," students will need instruction and practice in how to write an effective mathematical explanation that includes describing their problem-solving process using mathematical vocabulary. If students have never practiced this type of written explanation, they may not do well because they don't know how to write about math, which is different than if they can solve the problem or generate a solution. Explicitly teach students how to use the unfamiliar method and allow them time to practice and revise to get better at using it.

Many schools, districts, states, provinces, and national organizations have created documents to help guide the interpretation of standards. The Smarter Balanced Assessment Consortium (Smarter Balanced) and Partnership for Assessment of Readiness for College and Careers (PARCC) provide tools for assessing standards in terms of student work, and various states and provinces have developed their own versions of what methods will be used to assess the standards. Such organizations are striving to create a sense of coherence about what students and teachers working together need to achieve, as schools prepare students for a world we can scarcely imagine. These examples can provide ideas for classroom assessment. However, it is not recommended that every classroom assessment mirror these types of standardized items and tasks, as students tend to do poorly on standardized tests due to the fatigue of seeing the same type of item over and over again, and often they do not transfer their learning to new situations or know how to reasonably respond to something they are unfamiliar with (Allensworth et al., 2008; Wiggin, 2014; Wiliam, 2007). Classroom assessment needs to be varied in method or type and tightly aligned to the learning goal (Stiggins, 2005).

In determining the best method, given your context and learning goal, refer to table 3.1 (page 40), which describes the strengths and challenges of various methods.

Table 3.1: Strengths and Challenges of Various Assessment Methods

Methods	Strengths	Challenges	Sample Learning Goals
Selected Response: Multiple choice, true or false, matching, short answer	Selected response potentially offers some sense of why students do not understand when they mark an incorrect answer. Distracters or choices may be useful in determining something about student understanding or misunderstanding. Selected response can be used to efficiently get data on simple and some medium learning goals.	Students can guess easily. Selected response takes time to write or choose well (if finding items from another source).	I can identify coins and their values. I can add money.
Essay and Constructed Response: Construct a solution, justify a problem-solving method, or respond to a prompt or scenario	Constructed response allows for a deeper insight into how students are constructing meaning or gaining understanding. With a scoring guide, the expectations of these items are clear.	Students must be able to write well enough to communicate ideas, so this must be built into instruction so the summative assessment is not the first time learners independently write like this. Scoring takes more time. Sometimes the first few essays scored are looked at differently than the last few, because teachers get clearer about a quality response after reading a few.	I can use what I know about coins to solve real-world problems. I can make a model for my solution. I can construct an argument supporting the process I used to solve the problem. I can critique another mathematician's solution.
Performance Assessment: Produce, present, or perform—for instance, writing a paper, writing and responding to a weblog, preparing or presenting a speech or presentation, participating in dialogue, producing a video or audio clip	Performance assessment provides deep insight into how students are constructing meaning and are able to use it in authentic situations. These are often engaging tasks that, when written well, are naturally intriguing. There is often a specified audience that raises the level of concern and creates a more authentic situation.	Carefully written performance assessments take time to construct and time for students to create. Building in ample time is essential. Any work done at home may have the influence of those who have more support and can muddy the waters of what students are able to independently produce.	I can use what I know about money to solve problems and make decisions.

Table 3.2 shows methods that can work best for learning goals at various cognitive levels. However, context matters. That is to say, what students have experienced in the classroom can influence the actual level of cognition. Let's say the goal is to analyze figurative language and its impact on literary themes, and the students have analyzed Fitzgerald's (1926) use of winter in his short story "Winter Dreams." If asked the next day to write an essay detailing Fitzgerald's use of winter, students are no longer analyzing; they are explaining and recalling the analysis from the day before. The prompt would have to ask students to either use a different concept altogether or read a different text offering another use of winter and write a comparative essay.

Table 3.2: Methods That Reflect Learning Goals for Various Cognitive Levels

Complexity	Possible Student Work That Reflects the Learning Goal
Complex: Requires students to create or produce something new that synthesizes content and reasoning, often the work of the discipline—the work of scientists, mathematicians, artists, literary critics, mechanics, executives, accountants, geographers, professors, teachers, architects, lobbyists, counselors, and such	Products or performances, which include formal papers, debates, presentations, speeches, weblog posts, websites, movies, podcasts, flyers, brochures, proposals to introduce a solution to some authentic problem (for example, energy pollution, character dilemma)
Medium: Requires application or making sense of content and connecting to new situations or new understanding	Products or performances Constructed response, which includes explanations and problem solving Selected response, which includes some multiple choice, with students explaining their choices, or multiple choice that occurs in a series in which the questions build on each other
Simple: Requires students to recall or know where to find information on content or process	Multiple choice Short answer Matching (for identifying or recognizing)

Determine the Weight and Number of Items for Each Learning Goal

In the final step (which corresponds with the third and fourth columns on the assessment plan template; see figure 3.1, page 36), teachers determine the weight of each learning goal—much like a test specification chart that describes how many items will appear on the test for each assessed standard. During this step, consider the overall goal for your students; this is where the most weight should fall. For example, in the American dream unit, the goals of using evidence from the text to summarize, describing the central idea, and analyzing themes are most essential, and so they are worth forty points. The other area of emphasis focuses on multiple perspectives and comparing and contrasting those perspectives. Those learning goals are worth twenty-five points. Identifying key details in the text is least important on this summative assessment and is worth only eighteen points. In this step, we are intentionally deciding where we want students to spend most of their time and energy. This example uses points and percentages. In some cases, it might be more useful to use only percentages and indicate how many items or tasks will be included on the assessment. Often, the more complex the learning goal, the fewer the items and tasks you will need to create, but the more time and energy students will spend engaging in them. Percentages work best in this case, as they offer important information about how students have achieved the intended learning. The weight and the total-number columns ensure that the assessment has a good balance of items and tasks that reflect the kind of engaging work we want students to achieve.

For learning goals that have a simple or medium level of complexity, the rule of thumb is that four to six items per learning goal provide enough of a sample to determine student proficiency (Gareis & Grant, 2008). The most complex learning goals are most often larger tasks that require criteria or rubrics to assess quality. Often one or two tasks or prompts are sufficient to gather information on a student's proficiency. Any given assessment provides inferences only on a student's proficiency or understanding, so teachers must use the suggested number of items as a guideline. As new evidence emerges that shows a different level of proficiency, they must take that into account in reporting achievement at any given time.

If the school or classroom context is using standards-based reporting, assessments may be scored using those descriptors, so the learning goals are organized by the levels described in the standards-based system, and items indicate the work that shows if students have demonstrated that level (figure 3.2).

	Learning Goals	Method	Total Number of Items or Weight
4 **Exceeding Standard**	I can critique another mathematician's solution.	Students will get another student's solution (after the initial assessment) and offer feedback on what works about the solution and what the student could consider in doing it again.	1 item
3 **Meeting Standard**	I can construct an argument supporting the process I used to solve the problem.	Students will explain how they got their solution. Part of the criteria will be to use money vocabulary.	Explains 3 of the 6 problems
	I can make a model for my solution.	Students will create a number sentence as part of their solution.	Makes models for 1 item
	I can use what I know about coins to solve real-world problems.	Students will use what they know about money to respond. A possible topic is candy and friends.	Solves 3 items
2 **Approaching Standard**	I can add money. I can identify coins and their values.	Students get a bag of fake coins. They scoop up a handful of coins, draw the coins, and then add them up.	6 items
		Students use a word bank to name the coin from a picture and write its value (short answer).	4 items
1 **Beginning Understanding**	With support, I can complete the assessment.	Teacher guides students in understanding the task and asks questions to help the students solve the problems.	

Figure 3.2: Assessment plan for second-grade money unit using standards-based marks.

This type of intentional planning can not only increase the quality and engagement of our classroom assessments, it can also create great communication with students. Consider giving the assessment plan to students so that they can reflect on which of the goals they believe they understand and which they need to work on. Students might even develop items and tasks for each learning goal as a review before a summative task or test. A teacher could also cogenerate an assessment plan with students prior to the unit, creating opportunities for students to deeply invest in their own learning. This might also constitute an interesting action research project for educators looking for ways to increase student motivation and achievement. Such a project could study how student motivation and achievement are affected when the assessment is cogenerated, and how they differ from other units that are teacher created.

Choosing an appropriate method of assessment can aid in engagement and help both students and teachers connect the smaller learning goals that can sometimes feel fragmented and irrelevant without a bigger context and deeper meaning. For example, learning the five themes of geography (location, place, environment, movement, and region) may not seem that relevant to students. However, when asked to consider a cell phone company placing a tower near a small town in Wyoming, students could examine how the five themes factor into the cell phone company's decision. Combining two methods—a test on the five themes of geography with a performance task that asks students to make recommendations to the company— creates a fuller picture of what students know and how they might use that information.

Identifying learning goals in a cognitive progression, such as the ladder, however, can sometimes lead to teaching concepts in a fragmented manner, and fragmentation can cause difficulty for long-term retention and relevance. Students actually learn by creating meaning along the way. While some students learn best part to whole, others learn better starting with the whole and then moving to parts (Gallas, 1994). Effective teachers are constantly considering *how* students are engaging, learning, and understanding and are constantly responding by modifying instruction, examples, and activities to help students develop deeper levels of understanding

> *Students who struggle with certain concepts may do better with an authentic situation than they do practicing addition or identifying the adjectives in sentences.*

on the most essential ideas. For instance, students who struggle with certain concepts may do better with an authentic situation than they do practicing addition or identifying the adjectives in sentences. With a clear plan that maps out the student learning goals and the type of student work that reflects achievement of these learning goals, students are set up for success as teachers intentionally plan and use formative assessments to help students practice and then achieve at high levels.

Put Phase Three Into Play

List the learning goals in the first column of the assessment plan. Be sure to include both the simple and more complex learning goals—taken from the ladder created in phase two—that you want students to learn and master. Next, determine the type of method or item to measure or reflect this learning goal. Remember, various methods work best for different learning goals and cognitive levels. Finally, identify the number of items for each learning goal, or the percentage of weight. Figure 3.3 (page 44) shows the assessment plan for the second-grade money unit. (Figure 3.2 shows the same learning goals but includes the standards-based marks that align to them.) Visit **go.solution-tree.com/assessment** to see how the learning goals for the second-grade money unit were derived from the standards in phase two and to listen to a screencast modeling phase three for a fifth-grade reading assessment.

Learning Goals	Method	Total Number of Items or Weight
I can critique another mathematician's solution.	Students will get another student's solution (after the initial assessment) and offer feedback on what works about the solution and what the student could consider in doing it again.	20
I can construct an argument supporting the process I used to solve the problem.	Students will explain how they got their solution. Part of the criteria will be to use money vocabulary.	
I can make a model for my solution.	Students will create a number sentence as part of their solution.	10
I can use what I know about coins to solve real-world problems.	Students will use what they know about money to respond. A possible topic is candy and friends.	30
I can add money.	Students get a bag of fake coins. They scoop up a handful of coins, draw the coins, and then add them up.	30
I can identify coins and their values.	Students use a word bank to name the coin from a picture and write its value (short answer).	10

Figure 3.3: Assessment plan for second-grade money unit.

Pause and Ponder

The following questions are designed to help individual teachers or teams focus on the essential ideas presented in this chapter.

- What is the purpose of the assessment plan?
- What are the first three phases in the Design in Five process and how do they work together to set up a quality assessment?
- How could the ideas and assessment planning template in phase three support developing high-quality summative assessments?
- How could the ideas and assessment planning template in phase three support developing high-quality formative assessments?
- Which protocols and templates best support your work? In what ways could they lead to meaningful and engaging assessment design?
- What must we do to increase the quality and rigor of our summative and formative assessments?
- What other resources or practices do we know about that support or counter these ideas?

Creating the Assessment and Gathering the Materials

What the best and wisest parent wants for his [or her] own child, that must the community want for all its children.

—John Dewey

What we ask students to do through our assessment items and performance tasks speaks to what we believe students *can* do and is part of how we communicate expectations. When educators have high expectations for students, student achievement, success, and confidence increase (Hattie, 2009; Reeves, 2007). A student's confidence level contributes to his or her achievement (Dweck, 2006; Guo, Connor, Yang, Roehrig, & Morrison, 2012; Reeves, 2007), and students who lack confidence may not put much effort into the assessment task itself.

Phase four in the Design in Five process is critical because it is in the design of high-quality assessment tasks that we communicate these high expectations to students. Not all students come ready and willing to engage in these tasks. Student confidence is built through well-planned formative assessment practices and instruction that offers students time to practice, revise, and see and to experience growth on essential standards. Student engagement and confidence are also built through designing rigorous and relevant items and tasks that are meaningful and engaging.

What is rigor, and how should it be applied to assessment design? There are many conceptions of rigor. The Council for Aid to Education (CAE) has developed innovative assessments to describe critical thinking and problem solving. It describes rigor in terms of the kind of tasks and work students need to be engaged in to be successful: "Students today can no longer rely solely on mastery of discipline-based information. They need to be able to analyze and evaluate information, solve problems, and communicate effectively. Beyond just accumulating facts, they must be able to access, structure, and use information" (CAE, 2014). Rigor, for the purposes of classroom assessment design, is not about quantity of items or the amount of time spent on homework but the quality of tasks required. Quality rigorous tasks involve our students in taking the concepts we want them to learn and asking them to—individually and in collaboration with peers—

evaluate, analyze, and problem solve. Rigor is about asking students to communicate their thinking through writing and speaking. How do students take what they know about adding and subtracting fractions and solve real-world problems? How do they use what they know about geometry to graph the river bottom, collect samples from the river, and determine water quality? When students are posed with challenging tasks that are meaningful, their motivation increases (Brophy, 2004; McMillan, 2013). Rigorous assessments have great potential to engage students, increase academic achievement, and create classrooms where students and teachers are incredibly proud of the work they are doing.

What is relevance, and how should it influence assessment design? Relevance involves application of concepts in different ways and situations. It is about generating wonder and interest in what we are asking students to learn. According to the International Center for Leadership in Education, "Relevance refers to learning in which students apply core knowledge, concepts, or skills to solve real-world problems" (Daggett, 2014, p. 4). Relevant learning tasks are set in a context and can be interdisciplinary. At the most basic level, relevance is personal and addresses how students might relate to or use this concept in their own life. There is some merit to this response, but it is limiting and focuses too much on teachers having to make the content fun and can lead to surface-level connections. Relevance, at its best, is rooted in curiosity and the interesting aspects of the work. While relevant tasks can be fun, fun is not the central purpose. Relevance is about curiosity, application, and interest. As Ziegler (2008) notes, "Curiosity leads to open-mindedness and critical thinking, qualities every educator should want students to possess and develop" (p. 518). Relevance inspires meaningful questions and a genuine sense of students wondering about something—that may or may not directly influence their own experience. Relevance in assessment design is about generating high-quality, interesting, and engaging questions that tap the passion in a body of content. Ziegler (2008) also notes, "All that most topics really require to make them interesting to others is a teacher who exudes a fascination and interest in the topic. If a teacher does not show excitement, interest, and pleasure in the topics they cover, that lack will undoubtedly hinder student engagement" (p. 518). Relevant assessment design provides students with contexts—situations, scenarios, or roles—that are interesting and meaningful. Students may take on the role of a scientist or a literary critic or respond to scenarios that involve learning from past historical events. Relevant assessments are framed around the really interesting aspects of what is to be learned. During phase one of the Design in Five process, teachers plan engagement. This is where that engagement appears—through the tasks and items that are designed.

This chapter offers strategies for writing and revising quality assessment items, tasks, and rubrics that are rigorous and relevant. The guidelines and templates included provide a way for teachers to talk about and improve assessment tasks and items while also considering how students may experience them. If a student takes one look at the assessment—the structure, content, items, and task—and is overwhelmed or completely confused, the chance of getting good information about his or her level of understanding is unlikely. This reduces the strength of any inference we make about student learning (see the discussion of assessment validity in chapter 3, p. 35).

Phase four involves the nuts and bolts of quality-item, task, and rubric design for both validity and reliability. This phase has two steps.

1.   Create or revise assessment items and tasks for each learning goal.

2.   Develop student documents and gather necessary materials.

Create or Revise Assessment Items and Tasks for Each Learning Goal

To begin phase four of the design process, refer back to your assessment plan. For each learning goal, you will be creating the actual items and tasks you outlined in the plan. At this point, it is helpful to have other curriculum resources at your fingertips—bring your current texts and online resources to the table. The appendix provides a list of websites organized by level and content (page 129 and at **go.solution-tree.com /assessment**) that are particularly useful in sparking ideas for creating and revising items. Web links change, so creating your own list is most beneficial.

General Item and Task Characteristics

In choosing or creating items and tasks for each learning goal addressed on the assessment plan (phase three), consider the following three elements.

1. The alignment between item or task and learning goal. (This addresses validity.)

2. The cognitive level of the item or task. (This addresses rigor.)

3. The context that sets up the item or task. (This addresses relevance.)

The Alignment Between Item or Task and Learning Goal

The alignment between the item or task and the learning goal is key to getting good information about student understanding. As teachers write or find items, it is important to ask the question, "What does this item require students to know and do?" Sometimes we may assume that students are able to write a well-crafted essay or, because they are savvy technology users, that they understand how to design an effective presentation using some exotic new application. Paying attention to the skills students must have to achieve success on the item or task is essential. In this phase, we must double-check that students have learned how to effectively use the assessment method to show their understanding, make their argument, or accomplish the task as designed.

The Cognitive Level of the Item or Task

The second important element of an effective item or task is a clear connection to the intended cognitive level required by any given standard. Is the item at the level required by the standard and appropriate for the grade, content, and course? Students will achieve only the level that we provide them the opportunity to engage with. That is why we must be sure the assessment we offer is on target, on standard, and on grade level.

Table 4.1 (page 48) shows an example of matching methods and items to various cognitive levels using the American dream unit. These cognitive levels are based on Bloom's taxonomy; teachers may revise them to reflect their own list of cognitive levels. This process of examining the cognitive level in items is directly related to rigor. Tasks that asks students to apply, analyze, and problem solve are more rigorous than those that ask students to identify, define, or recognize.

Table 4.1: Assessment Tasks Per Cognitive Level

Cognitive Levels	Methods	Sample Items, Tasks, and Prompts
Evaluation: *Appraise, argue, assess, attach, choose, compare, defend, estimate, judge, predict, rate, select, support, value, evaluate*	• Presentations • Projects • Scenarios	Assess the poem "Dreaming America" (Oates, 1973) and the significance of winter in the short story "Winter Dreams" by Fitzgerald (1926).
Synthesis: *Arrange, assemble, collect, compose, construct, create, design, develop, formulate, manage, organize, plan, prepare, propose, set up, write*	• Presentations • Projects • Scenarios • Products • Plans	In what ways does "Dreaming America" capture the same meaning of the concept of winter, as represented in "Winter Dreams"? In what ways is it different? Use evidence from the text and explanations of your interpretation to construct your response.
Analysis: *Analyze, appraise, calculate, categorize, compare, contrast, criticize, differentiate, discriminate, distinguish, examine, experiment, question, test*	• Graphs • Essays • Projects • Scenarios	Examine this quote: "Dexter was unconsciously dictated to by his winter dreams" (Fitzgerald, 1926, p. 46). What is the significance of this quote? Explain your response, and use examples and citations from the text to support your response.
Application: *Apply, choose, demonstrate, dramatize, employ, illustrate, interpret, operate, practice, schedule, sketch, solve, use, write*	• Essays • Some multiple choice • Plans • Storyboards	In Joyce Carol Oates's (1997) interview she describes Americans as "idealistic." In "Dreaming America," describe the ways in which Oates's notion of idealism plays out and does not play out. Interpret specific parts of the poem to support your response.
Comprehension: *Classify, describe, discuss, explain, express, identify, indicate, locate, recognize, report, restate, review, select, translate*	• Short answers • Essays • Multiple choice	Describe the setting of the short story "Winter Dreams."

Visit **go.solution-tree.com/assessment** or page 142 for a blank reproducible form of this figure.

The wording (especially the verb) of learning goals provides one interpretation of the cognitive level, but the work students are asked to complete, produce, create, or engage in determines the actual cognitive level. Table 4.2 shows how this works in practice. The first column articulates the learning goal. The next column shows student work that tends to oversimplify the goal. The final column describes work that meets the rigor of the learning goal.

Table 4.2: Oversimplified Work Versus Work That Meets the Rigor of the Learning Goal

Learning Goal	Oversimplified Interpretation of the Learning Goal	Intended Cognitive Level of the Learning Goal
I can summarize text.	This assessment task interprets *summarize* as identifying characteristics. *Which of the following best describes the main character, Dexter, in "Winter Dreams"?* A. Dreamy B. Determined C. Angry D. Caring	This assessment task interprets *summarize* as part of determining the main idea and explaining why. *Which of the following statements best describes the main idea of the text?* A. Money doesn't buy happiness. B. Determination is the way to achieve your dreams. C. Relationships with the wrong people can squelch a dream. D. Dreams desired may bring with them unexpected consequences. *Explain why you think so, and use evidence from the story to support your opinion.*
I can demonstrate an understanding of quadratics and exponent rules.	This assessment task interprets the learning goal to mean students will solve quadratic equations. *Solve the following quadratic using any two of the methods we have learned this year (graphing, factoring, completing the square, quadratic formula).* $0 = 2x^2 + 12x + 16$	This assessment task interprets the learning goal to mean students can use quadratic equations to solve problems. *A motorboat is moving upstream and downstream on a river. The motorboat makes a round trip on the river 56 miles upstream and 56 miles downstream, maintaining a constant speed of 15 miles per hour relative to the water. The entire trip up and back takes 7.5 hours. What is the speed of the current? (ikleyn, n.d.)* *Explain how quadratics help solve this problem.*
I can apply what I know about grammar.	This assessment task interprets the learning goal to mean students will be able to identify parts of speech and correct a mistake. *Identify the part of speech in a sentence.* *Correct or revise language usage errors in a text.*	This assessment task interprets the learning goal to mean students will apply their understanding of grammar through actually writing and revising. *Think about a character in Gary Paulsen's book* Hatchet. *Describe the character and use examples from the text to support your descriptions.* *Write a draft. In class, we will consider characteristics of quality writing. Then you will revise your writing one more time; fixing run-on sentences and fragments.*
I can analyze how different countries respond in economic crises.	This assessment task interprets the learning goal to mean students will be able to identify how a country might respond. *Which of the following best describes how Greece handled its economic crisis?* *Which of the following explains the similarities between Greece and the United States in terms of their handling of economic crises?*	This assessment task interprets the learning goal to mean students will actually analyze the similarities and differences among countries' responses to economic crises. This also means that this analysis has not occurred in class. *Write an essay analyzing the similarities and differences between how Greece and the United States handled their economic crises. Use evidence from the three articles we read in class to make your case.*

Teachers must also consider the difficulty and complexity of each assessment. Difficulty refers to how hard something might be, while complexity describes the kind of cognitive demand involved, essentially what we are considering rigor. For example, an assessment may be more difficult if there are more problems to work or more questions to answer; quantity has more to do with difficulty than complexity. Difficult tasks involve time spent replicating, recalling, and performing routine tasks. When tasks are more complex, the time is spent analyzing, creating, synthesizing, and digging into fewer tasks with more depth—often showing relationships among concepts, ideas, and texts and then making sense of the process used as well as the insight gained. Table 4.3 shows these differences.

Table 4.3: Difficulty Versus Complexity

Learning Goal	Difficult	Complex
I can interpret, describe, and create graphs for various situations.	Answering questions or making inferences about many graphs	Generating a graph based on data to support transportation changes that reduce pollution
I can use what I know about addition to solve problems.	Adding double-digit and triple-digit numbers; providing word problems with the same problem-solving process needed	Creating situations or scenarios where addition is necessary to solve problems
I can describe the approaches authors make in their text.	Answering a multiple-choice item that asks students to identify the best explanation of the author's approach	Providing a short response identifying the approach (either from a list or not) and then using evidence from the text to justify and illustrate their position
I can identify and apply what I know about shapes.	Identifying circles from a bunch of shapes Identifying circles in a photograph of the New York City skyline	Viewing a photograph that contains circles and answering the question, *How would the place and experience change if there were no circles, or if the circles were now squares?*
I can analyze ideas from multiple perspectives.	Answering a question that asks for an opinion, such as, *Do you agree with what the story says about women? Explain.*	Answering a question that asks students to consider various texts, such as, *Provide two texts that portray women differently. How does each story portray women? Use evidence from the text to support your argument.*

In any assessment that is seeking to understand the extent to which students can independently engage in the learning goal, the task must be novel—something that has not been discussed or considered before.

After teasing out the cognitive demand, consider how to craft items and tasks to ensure alignment to the learning goal. For example, to accomplish a true analysis of irony, students would need to discuss or analyze irony in a new literary piece, not one that had previously been discussed. Students might also compare and contrast the use of irony in multiple literary pieces. Even more boldly, you could ask them to look at how irony is used in an informational text. This is the kind of deep thinking that pushes students to consider not only the role of irony in literature, but how it is used in a variety of contexts. In any assessment that is seeking to understand the extent to which students can independently engage in the learning goal, the task must be novel—something that has not been discussed or considered before. However, the summative assessment must *not* be the first time students have to independently analyze or solve a problem. Students need practice in attacking novel situations so they can learn the process of what Wiliam (2013) calls the only 21st century skill: knowing what to do when you encounter a situation you have not seen before.

The Context That Sets up the Item or Task

The third element of an effective item or task is a relevant and meaningful context—that is the *why* of the learning, as identified in phase one. In other words, how do these topics appear within the world of the discipline? How are they used, adapted, or created by scientists, mathematicians, authors, plumbers, artists, managers, doctors, nurses, or teachers? In an authentic situation, learning goals create relevance, and the audience for the learner's work is more than the teacher. For instance, a student might write a critique of literature and present his or her critique to a group of peers or post it online to receive responses that support or counter his or her position. Students might take on the role of a character to describe the events in a novel. Or, they might write or present as the scientist who performed an investigation and made a life-changing discovery. Whether the audience is someone other than the teacher or students taking on a new role, setting the context can provide an engaging and relevant scenario for students to learn and grow.

The general considerations for designing items and tasks provide direction for high-quality assessment practices. Consider the following questions when applying these general design characteristics to creating or revising assessment items.

- What is the learning goal that is being assessed in this item or task? Does this item reflect the meaning of the standard or learning goal?

- What is the cognitive level of this item or task? How rigorous is it?

- How is this item or task relevant? Is the context of the item interesting or the role students play relevant? Does the item or task promote critical thinking and curiosity?

The rigor and relevance of any given item or task is dependent on the context and the purpose of the assessment. The next four sections provide characteristics for specific types, including constructed-response tasks, performance assessments, rubrics, and multiple-choice items.

Quality Characteristics of Constructed-Response Tasks

The definition of *constructed response* is not clearly articulated in the field (Hogan, 2013). For the purpose of this design process, constructed response is defined as any item or task that requires students to construct their own response to a situation, question, or problem. This response may be to recall information and explain it in their own words, which would be a lower-cognitive-level task. For example, an item such as, "Explain the major causes of World War II" asks students to recall causes that were discussed in class and read about in a text. A constructed-response task might also be at a higher cognitive level, such as providing students with data about the technology use of fourth graders and asking them to generate a summary of what the data say and suggest possible actions teachers might take to capitalize on technology use in classrooms.

A review of student work and how students respond on each item or task provides information about the effectiveness of any given item.

The response to each task provides information about the effectiveness of any given item. Have you ever had an item on a test that more than half the students answered incorrectly, and when looking back, it was clear the students' misinterpretation of the item was to blame, not a lack of understanding? This type of interrogation of student responses is a strong way to effectively revise constructed-response tasks.

Consult the following list for support and direction in writing quality constructed-response items. (Visit **go.solution-tree.com/assessment** to download this in the form of a checklist you can use in your teams to revise assessment tasks.)

- Consider the learning goal and the standard. Check the verb in the prompt and ensure it aligns to the standards and the level of thinking required. For example, *identify* might signal that students can name an example of a chemical reaction, whereas *describe* means students must add evidence that explains the characteristics that make it a chemical reaction.

- Provide context and background information that is relevant to setting up the question. This may include using a quote from a text, a statement about the content, or the topic of focus.

- Avoid general questions. For example, "Of all the novels we have read, which one do you like best, and why?" or "Which law has had the most impact on our economy? Explain your choice." Such questions leave the door open for surface-level and vague responses.

- Avoid options within the question. Although choice offers students some apparent sense of control, what they are called upon to do may vary cognitively. For example, in one social studies assessment, students were asked to write two essays from among four options. Two were at a comprehension level, and two were focused on analysis. I'm sure you can imagine which two were most often selected.

- Carefully set up the logistics of the assessment, and clearly communicate the time frame and process, including any revision guidelines.

- Provide clear instructions and steps that will enable students to successfully engage in the assessment.

- If using some type of device (for example, iPad, smartphone, computer), be sure the equipment is easily accessible and that students are comfortable using the application or device.

- Review and remove extraneous or misleading information.

- Make wording clear and remove extra phrases and redundant words. Sometimes, for the sake of clarity, we provide too much detail. In addition, sometimes words that students are unfamiliar with are used. Be sure to explicitly teach vocabulary needed to form a well-thought-out and accurate response.

- Use multiple methods for constructed responses: A response may come in the form of a written essay, an audio recording, or a graphic organizer. Students construct their own graphic organizer to show understanding and relationships of ideas or teachers may provide a graphic organizer for students to complete.

- Check items for unintended bias or stereotyping. How are racial, ethnic, religious, gender, and social groups portrayed? Are there cultural phrases, concepts, or experiences that have not been taught or learned that students will need to be familiar with to engage in the assessment? Be sure to review student responses and throw out any items or tasks that unfairly assume students have had a particular experience.

- Establish scoring criteria in advance.

- Set guidelines about how factors that may influence performance but not directly taught will be included (that is, writing or presentation skills).

- Score anonymously, if possible.

Figure 4.1 shows an example of planning for a constructed-response prompt for the ninth-grade American dream unit.

Learning goal: I can compare and contrast key messages in multiple texts on the same topic.	
Provide background and context.	We have been exploring the following question: How has the American dream changed over time? We have read "I Hear America Singing" by Walt Whitman (1860) and "Winter Dreams" by F. Scott Fitzgerald (1926). We have also read a survey on the American dream (Center for the Study of the American Dream, 2014).
Craft the question or task—be sure the cognitive level is clear.	For this task, read "Dreaming America," by Joyce Carol Oates (1973), and view the NBC news clip describing and questioning the state of the American dream (www.nbcnews.com/feature/in-plain-sight/state-american-dream-uncertain-v19306579). Given the information in the article and the video, describe the key messages and how they develop. Explain your thinking using evidence from the text and video. In addition, compare and contrast the two pieces, again using evidence to support your thinking.
Create or provide a scoring guide.	Consider the following in writing your response. • Maintain a focus on a general topic, and attempt a focus on a specific issue. • Present a thesis establishing a general focus on the topic. • Develop the topic by selecting well-chosen, relevant, and sufficient support. • Use adequate language to communicate: correct grammar, usage, and mechanics, with few distracting errors that do not impede understanding. • Use appropriate vocabulary. • Use varied sentence structures to vary pace.

Figure 4.1: Planning a constructed-response prompt for the ninth-grade American dream unit.

Figure 4.2 (page 54) shows an elementary school example of planning for a constructed-response prompt for the second-grade money unit.

Learning Goals: I can use what I know about coins to solve real-world problems. I can make a model for my solution. I can construct an argument supporting the process I used to solve the problem.	
Provide background and context.	We have been studying money and the best ways to solve problems and represent solutions.
Craft the question or task—be sure the cognitive level is clear.	Provide a solution and explanation for the following problems. Sara loves chocolate. The candy bar costs 25 cents. Her friend, Tasha, loves Skittles. A bag costs 35 cents. How much money will it cost for the two treats? Draw the coins you would use to pay for these treats. Create a model to show your possible solution. Explain how you got your answer. Use words, pictures, or both.
Create or provide a scoring guide.	Note the criteria for this problem. • Explanations make sense and align with math work • Explanation uses mathematical vocabulary • Accurately solves problem and uses clear models

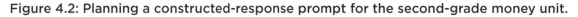

Figure 4.2: Planning a constructed-response prompt for the second-grade money unit.

Quality Characteristics of Performance Assessments

A performance assessment is a task in which we ask students to produce, present, or perform in an authentic context or real-world purpose—for example, by writing a paper or weblog; preparing or presenting a speech, video, or podcast; or more formally participating in dialogue or debate.

When designed, planned, and executed well, performance tasks have a natural way of helping students make meaning of concepts and find relevance in their work. A quality performance assessment has a clear audience and a purpose that is compelling for students, putting them in the position to contribute to the discipline or even provide solutions to local or global issues. Engaging in the performance task is not only about completing a class assignment or consuming ideas already established but also about producing knowledge or perspectives. Teachers design performance tasks on the most essential standards and create experiences focused on the learning goals they want students to remember beyond the course or grade level.

In a study of water quality, for example, students might write or present to the community, informing them about the state's water quality and offering suggestions to either improve or conserve it. Using their own data and studies from other researchers, students build a compelling case for the community to consider. The website Artsonia (www.artsonia.com) provides a place for students to share and explain their artwork. Other students can comment on original pieces of work from students all over the world. Consider the following when designing performance assessments.

- Establish an essential question or big idea that puts learning in context (tap into essential questions or engaging scenarios crafted in phase one). Heather Lattimer (2008) offers key elements for a history course by crafting challenging and meaningful tasks around big questions. Questions include: When is violence justified? Who should have access to the American dream? Are the benefits of progress worth the costs? Can we have both liberty and security? Students were challenged to use a text to build their argument.

- Address a concern and provide a solution or issue in the community. Performance tasks might provide solutions to a problem in the school or local community.

- Use the standards to inform and shape the task. The standards ask students to frame an argument using multiple sources and to provide counterarguments in some cases. Both of these sample criteria can aid in helping students craft a powerful message.

- Consider the medium or method carefully. If students have access to technology, they may be able to create an iMovie. Consider the instruction needed to engage in a medium like iMovie and the access students have to that type of technology. A PowerPoint presentation may capture some of the message, but when used poorly it becomes just another way to write a paper, with little benefit to putting ideas on multiple slides. If using writing, students must be taught to write for the specific purpose and audience.

- Prioritize the task and ensure it is achievable within the time frame and the context of class. Consider carefully the work outside of class. Parents who are able to spend the time and who have a related experience may offer more than a supportive comment or critique. The work can quickly turn into a partnership between student and parent. This may be helpful, except, of course, if the goal of the performance task is for students to independently demonstrate their understanding.

- Provide ample time for students to revise. Consider revision as part of instruction so that the issue of time is not seen as the biggest barrier to this type of task.

- Ensure that the task is culturally relevant and that the vocabulary and experience needed to achieve the task is accessible to and learned by all students.

- Avoid options that change the learning goals and level of complexity of the task.

- Provide a clear set of expectations criteria for the assessment task. Science teachers lament the use of flowery language in a lab report.

- Provide opportunities for students to self-assess on their learning and the process.

Table 4.4 shows a completed performance assessment task for the American dream unit.

Table 4.4: Completed Performance Assessment Plan for the American Dream Unit

Step 1. Establish the Learning Goals	
Identify the learning goals in your assessment plan (phase three).	I can use evidence from the texts I have read to generate dialogue.
Are there other skills or knowledge students might need to accomplish the task that may not have been explicitly taught? Plan how to support students so this doesn't become the reason they do not achieve.	I can produce an objective summary of a text.
	I can analyze the details that lead to the theme over the course of a text.
	I will also need to teach students how to record on the iPads, along with what constitutes a high-quality podcast.
Step 2. Set the Context	
What is the context of the task? What is the purpose of the task?	The context: A podcast or video cast
	Audience: National Public Radio
Who's the audience? Describe why they would care about this work.	Students' role: They have written a magazine article and are now being asked to do a podcast or video cast
What role do students play?	

Continued on next page →

Step 3. Design the Task	
Consider the cognitive level required and desired. Be sure that what students are required to do to complete the task meets the cognitive level.	A local radio station is doing a segment on the American dream. As journalists for a national magazine, students wrote an article on how the American dream has changed and what the current reality is for students leaving high school and college.
Frame the context.	
Frame the task, product, or presentation.	Record (audio or video) a statement that is six to eight minutes in length describing the change that has occurred and the reality that eighteen- to thirty-year-olds are facing today. Include how this new reality might influence you and your plans for the future.
Describe the form the product or presentation should take. This may be a place where students have options. Be careful that any options in form (writing, presenting, video, poster, and so on) do not change the learning goals.	

Step 4. Lay Out the Materials	
Make a checklist of materials needed to achieve this task. Ensure that students have access to tools and materials with no significant financial or resource burden.	Time in class to write and revise their podcast or video cast
	Socratic dialogue to develop their podcast or video cast
	Time in class to record

Step 5. Lay Out the Criteria	
Develop scoring guides and rubrics to clearly describe the criteria. Use general rubrics your school or district adopted as guidelines.	Clear and focused argument
	Developed argument (effective textual evidence that is explained well)
Consider co-constructing some of these criteria so students generate a clear vision of quality work.	Multiple sources
	Accurate interpretations of texts
	Effective language use

Visit **go.solution-tree.com/assessment** for a blank reproducible form of this table.

Quality Characteristics of Rubrics

Rubrics are descriptive tools that help create clear learning expectations for students—a foundational element of quality assessment practices. Easily understood rubrics, including those that students themselves have helped to create, become a great communication tool both for reporting summative scores as well as for formative work that provides students with information to improve and an opportunity for self-assessment (Brookhart, 2013a; Davies, 2007b). Rubrics describe the characteristics of student work at varying levels of achievement, usually in matrix form and with text or student work samples that show various stages of proficiency.

Rubrics are different from scoring checklists. Checklists indicate if an element is present or not, or if the work is simply right or wrong. Rubrics describe the quality of the work. Scoring checklists sometimes quantify elements, identifying how many things or examples need to be present, where rubrics describe the quality of those elements. There are two types of rubrics: *analytic* and *holistic*. Analytic rubrics break scores down by individual criteria, like the analytic rubric in figure 4.3, meaning students get one score for each criterion measured in the assessment task.

Criteria	Beginning	Emerging	Proficient	Distinguished
Mathematical explanations and vocabulary	Explanation is missing or incomplete.	Explanation describes the math work.	Explanation uses mathematical vocabulary and clearly describes the math work.	Explanation uses mathematical vocabulary and thoroughly describes the math work so others can replicate the process.
Problem solving	Student inaccurately solves problem.	Student accurately solves the problem.	Student accurately solves the problem and uses clear models.	Student accurately solves the problem and uses models to show relationships to the problem solving.

Figure 4.3: Analytic mathematics rubric.

Holistic rubrics provide one score for the whole product or presentation, usually describing multiple criteria, as shown in the rubric for a second-grade math unit (figure 4.4). Students must meet all criteria for a certain level to receive that score; otherwise, the score drops down a level.

4	Thoroughly explains problem-solving process so others can replicate the process
	Uses mathematical vocabulary to describe problem solving
	Accurately solves problem and uses models to show relationships to the problem solving
3	Explanation makes sense and aligns with math work
	Explanation uses mathematical vocabulary
	Accurately solves problem and uses clear models
2	Explains problem solving without using math terms
	Accurately solves problem
1	Explanation is missing or incomplete
	Inaccurately solves problem

Figure 4.4: Holistic second-grade mathematics rubric.

Students benefit from rubrics—especially when teachers intentionally use them as part of the instructional process. To develop a clear idea of quality, students begin by scoring anonymous examples of student work using the rubric. This prompts dialogue. Then, with a clearer idea of quality, students move to assessing and revising their own work based on their interpretations of the rubric. This sequence allows students to provide feedback to both peers and themselves. Susan Brookhart's (2013a) *How to Create and Use Rubrics for Formative Assessment and Grading* provides quality examples and additional compelling notes for designing rubrics.

Following are the elements of a quality rubric.

- The rubric describes student work at varying levels of quality, versus describing work as either right or wrong.

- The rubric does not quantify criteria. Use a combination of a checklist and a rubric to avoid descriptions like "one-to-two mistakes" or "three-to-five examples." The piece might have five examples, but what is the quality of those examples? A rubric should describe the quality of the descriptions; a checklist can be offered to address quantities when necessary.

- The rubric avoids descriptions that use words like *sometimes, always*, and *occasionally*. Instead, describe attributes of the quality of the work.

- The rubric describes clearly observable attributes of a product or performance.

- The rubric frames the descriptions and levels with positive language, describing what is present in the student work at each level versus what is not there, with a clear difference among levels. Use negative language sparingly. When framed positively, students can identify where their work falls on the rubric in order to advance to the next level. Instead of "lacks a claim and supporting details," which describe what is not present, a beginning-level description might read, "summarizes the text." The next level would then provide descriptions of how to move from a summary to "clearly states a claim and provides details in support of that claim." There are times when it is incredibly difficult to frame the beginning levels of a rubric with positive language. Student examples often help in crafting characteristics at the beginning levels. When crafting a writing rubric, a team of teachers gathered anonymous examples of student work and put them in order of quality. The student work in its beginning stages appeared to use basic vocabulary, and as the work increased in quality, more descriptive words were used. This informed the beginning description of word use on the writing rubric. This kind of language can help students describe their work and then, with a strong rubric, they can understand the action needed to make their work stronger by referencing the next level on the rubric.

- The rubric uses simple, descriptive, and concise language. The more text there is, the more complicated and hard to understand a rubric becomes. Rubrics are intended to provide clarity, but if they are cumbersome and difficult to interpret and use, they do not serve their purpose.

- The rubric uses an even number of levels of performance to avoid the middle being the catchall. Providing even levels requires a clear decision about the quality of the piece of work. The more levels of performance, the more sensitive the scoring. However, the more levels, the more complicated the scoring. Most classroom rubrics are effective when offering between four and six levels.

- The rubric can be used for various performance tasks or constructed responses over time. Having the whole rubric provides the big picture, but by using parts of the rubric with multiple tasks, problems, or writing, students begin to see connections to their work, revision, and improvement over time. For example, if there are three criteria in your lab-analysis rubric, consider having students self-assess on one criterion and then make revisions accordingly, or choose one criterion that, after scanning student work, seems most challenging for students to achieve. Offer a minilesson, and then provide time for revision on that one aspect of the rubric.

Individual teachers, teams of teachers, or teachers and students may use the following steps in crafting an effective rubric.

1. **Identify the standards and criteria to be assessed:** These are most often already articulated in the learning goals on your assessment plan developed in phase three. The rubric could also be used for a specific task or something students develop over time, such as writing, a lab analysis, a primary source critique, or a vocal or instrumental performance. For example, a writing standard includes multiple criteria, such as organization, content, mechanics, and so on. A science inquiry standard includes multiple criteria, such as data analysis, data representation, conclusions, and implications.

2. **Determine the number of levels:** The more levels, the more accurate the score. However, the more levels, the more complex the rubric is to understand and use. You may want to consider using the number of levels represented on your standards-based report card (if applicable). Otherwise, four to six levels are generally the most manageable and the most effective for classroom assessment use.

3. **Describe the levels of achievement:**

   a. Start with one criterion and write statements that describe what students achieve when they have met the standard. This becomes language for level three on a four-point scale. Pay particular attention to the verbs in the standard as this is what should be reflected at level three; this is the minimum level we want all students to achieve.

   b. If you have examples of student work available, remove the names from the work and order the samples from best to worst. Write statements that describe attributes of the work, describing what is there versus what is not. This will help keep your rubric framed positively.

   c. Then, describe levels two and one, which represent the basic knowledge students must display to achieve the standard. You might want to look at student work that reflects a one or two and describe what is present.

   d. Finally, describe what the learning looks like at its most complex level, or level four. At this level, students should display higher levels of thinking. Don't get too bogged down in choosing words in this step; once you start using the rubric with student work, areas that need revision will become clear. It is one thing to design a rubric, but another to use it. In actually applying the language you have created to student work samples, the revisions to the rubric come naturally.

4. **Revise the language to better reflect the qualities of student work:** As you use the rubric over time, collect exemplars at every level for student and teacher use. These exemplars will help provide clarity around expectations for instruction and assessment on the standards in the rubric.

The sample Socratic dialogue rubric in figure 4.5 (page 60) was designed to score the dialogue for the ninth-grade American dream unit assessment. The rubric was constructed using learning goals from the assessment plan (indicated by italics in the table); some of the more basic learning goals provide language for the beginning and emerging levels, and the more complex learning goals inform the proficient and distinguished levels.

Collaboration is an important process often used in instruction to dig deeper into new learning. Caution must be taken when assessing achievement through collaboration. It is recommended that students produce some independent work to describe achievement and report collaboration separately. It is hard to determine from a collaboratively created product the level of understanding students bring to the table. Working together and collaborating to solve problems and generate innovative solutions is an essential aspect of success beyond high school and in whatever career path students choose to pursue. As we frame tasks for students through collaboration, consider how to assess collaboration separately from other achievement indicators. Mixing them together can lead to frustrated students and inaccurate information regarding a

Criteria	1 Beginning	2 Emerging	3 Proficient	4 Distinguished
Questioning	I can ask questions to clarify what the text means.	I can pose questions that reference the text.	I can pose questions that emerge directly from text evidence. I can pose questions to clarify a peer's contribution.	I can use multiple contributions to pose deeper-level questions.
Expressing ideas	*I can produce an objective summary of a text.*	I can express my ideas clearly with loose connections to the text.	I can express my ideas clearly and persuasively using text evidence. I can summarize points of agreement and disagreement.	I can make new connections from evidence and reasoning in the dialogue.
Generating ideas	I can reiterate what someone else said.	I can respond to questions in a dialogue.	*I can use evidence from the texts I have read to generate dialogue.* I can build on others' ideas.	I can pose questions and comments that help the dialogue go deeper.

Figure 4.5: Socratic dialogue rubric.

Visit **go.solution-tree.com/assessment** for a reproducible form of this figure.

student's understanding of individual standards. The rubric for assessing collaborative work (figure 4.6) provides guidance in describing quality collaboration and can be used as a separate criteria in any collaborative assessment task.

Some rubrics are designed to provide vertical and system alignment as well as to inform classroom assessment work. A college-and-career-readiness design team in the Spring Lake Park Schools in Minnesota identified writing as one of the key skills critical to student success and readiness for success beyond high school. They realized that elevating writing to be included in benchmark assessment data would help make this critical skill a higher priority and bring greater attention to students writing in many different contexts. To this end, the team established writing benchmarks at grades 4, 7, and 10 to check progress and writing instruction. Rubrics were designed in the following grade bands: K–3, 4–5, 6–8, and 9–12. Teams of teachers within each grade band met and developed writing rubrics around the same four criteria: focus, development, organization, and language use. The rubric language was informed by the state writing standards to ensure that the levels described the increasing sophistication required for high-quality writing. In addition, each level is collecting exemplars. These rubrics not only provide the scoring mechanism for those more formal benchmarks, they also provide teachers with criteria and rubrics to use in their ongoing classroom assessment work in all content areas.

Grades 7 and 10 teacher teams design their respective writing benchmark tasks, and the department scores the work. This collaborative scoring process increases teacher understanding of writing and provides more clarity around writing expectations. Visit **go.solution-tree.com/assessment** for the accompanying Spring Lake Park K-12 writing rubric.

Criteria	Trying	Striving	Thriving
Listening	Listens to ideas with some interruptions or repeating of ideas	Listens to ideas with nonverbal and verbal acknowledgment (eye contact, body language)	Listens to ideas, paraphrases ideas, and builds and makes connections to ideas
Contributing	Offers a few thoughts to the group	Offers thoughts to the group that are on topic Helps the group achieve its task, product, or dialogue	Puts ideas on the table Makes connections to specific texts, resources, or activities Pushes the group to accomplish a task, product, or dialogue that everyone feels proud of
Questioning	May ask a few questions to clarify	Asks questions to clarify the task or understand another person's ideas	Asks questions to clarify the task and understand another's ideas, especially when they don't agree Asks questions that lead to spirited and meaningful dialogue and ideas

Figure 4.6: Rubric for assessing collaborative work.

Quality Characteristics of Multiple-Choice Items

Multiple-choice items were first developed and used by Frederick J. Kelly in 1914, arising from concerns about variability in the way that teachers score work and the amount of time it took to do so (Davidson, 2011). Interestingly, Kelly seems later to shift his stance on the effectiveness of multiple-choice items for assessment. He was clearly concerned with the lack of critical thinking present in the trends of the time and advocated for a more balanced approach that required more thinking on the part of students. However, by that time, the United States had embraced the notion of efficiency in testing (Davidson, 2011).

There is a time and a place for multiple choice if used with balance and intention. They are best used to understand students' ability to recall, identify, and, in some cases, evaluate and analyze. When designed well, they can help us understand student misconceptions, generate dialogue, and inform instruction (Wiliam, 2011). When designed poorly, they frustrate students and provide inaccurate evidence to teachers. See figure 4.7 (page 62 and online) for a blank template that will assist in writing effective multiple-choice items.

Multiple choice remains one of the predominant ways students are assessed in a standardized format in K–12 schooling, as well as in many entrance exams for careers and colleges. Innovations in the design, format, and sequence of multiple-choice items have made them more rigorous and thus more useful in creating efficient and effective ways of understanding what students know and can do. However, they are limited in their ability to reveal what is working in terms of instruction and what needs to happen next.

Because many high-stakes assessments use multiple-choice items, educators often feel that if students are to do well, classroom assessments should reflect this form. In fact, the opposite seems to be true. When students see too many multiple-choice items, they often do not do as well. Sometimes they are fatigued from

Phase Four. Multiple Choice Template

Writing a multiple-choice item requires intentional design of the stem (question), the distracters (plausible choices that tell you about student's misunderstanding), and the key (the correct answer). Use the quality characteristics of multiple-choice items on pages 63–66 to craft your items. Use the template to below to ensure high-quality distracters.

Stem:		
What is the main idea the author wants the reader to understand?		
	Statement	Misconception
A.	Feral dogs are generally dangerous	An isolated fact
B.	Diclofenac given to livestock is killing vultures	Contributes to the problem
C.	The extinction of vultures is not good for humans.	Correct! Main idea supported by A, B, and D
D.	Vultures are an important part of the Parsi burial ritual	Support for why extinction is not good
Stem:		
	Statement	Misconception
A.		
B.		
C.		
D.		
Stem:		
	Statement	Misconception
A.		
B.		
C.		
D.		

Figure 4.7: Multiple choice template.

this type of assessment or don't see its relevance to their learning. Or, students may begin to think that they need to memorize or recall everything to do well. And when students used to multiple-choice assessments get to something they don't know, they can't think about it, reason, and select the best possible choice (Allensworth et al., 2008; Wiggins, 2014; Wiliam, 2007).

However, multiple-choice items can be written and used well. A well-written multiple-choice item consists of three parts: (1) the *stem* is the question or the statement that sets up the question or the desired response;

(2) the *key* is the right answer; and (3) the *distracters* are the plausible choices that indicate misconception or level of understanding.

Following are characteristics to consider when writing the stem (Davidson, 2011; Gareis & Grant, 2008; Little, Bjork, Bjork, & Angello, 2012; Stiggins et al., 2004).

- **If providing context in the stem, attempt to limit it to no more than four lines:** If there are more than four lines, insert a paragraph break to set the question apart from the context.

- **Be sure the majority of the text is in the stem, not the distracters:** Having multiple choices with dense texts most often makes the item more difficult but not more complex.

- **Ask a full question in the stem (for example, "Which of the following best describes the main idea of the text?"):** Attempt to avoid statements that call for completion in the distracters (for example, The main idea of this paragraph is . . .). Students, especially English as a second language learners and younger students, can hold a question longer than they can hold a statement. If they have to go back and reread the stem, there is more chance for error in interpreting it. If you are using a statement that requires completion, make sure the blanks are the same length. Students will try to compare the length of the blanks with the distracters, increasing the chances they get it right or wrong for a reason other than whether they know or don't know the answer.

- **Ensure that vocabulary in the stem and distracters is clear and familiar to students:** Be sure vocabulary is understood and familiar. Being aware of cultural language patterns is essential, as the vocabulary used and the way sentences or questions are framed can support or hinder a student's understanding of the question. When selecting or revising questions from multiple sources, it is easy to overlook terms that are unfamiliar.

- **State the question in the positive whenever possible:** In other words, avoid "Which one of these is *not* a maple leaf?" Steven J. Burton, Richard R. Sudweeks, Paul F. Merrill, and Bud Wood (1991) find that students get this kind of frame wrong more often, because the brain is wired to find the connection, not the absence of the connection. You are probably thinking that standardized tests use this frame all the time. However, most standardized test items have been field-tested and revised over time according to patterns seen from lumping multiple items together. We don't have that luxury in classroom assessment practices. Try using "select all that apply" if you need to modify the question—in which case, students would select more than one choice. There is a time and a place to teach students how to interpret test items, but test-taking preparation does not have to be embedded in every assessment throughout the year.

- **Highlight critical words (*most, only, except, best*) using bold or capital letters:** Avoid italics and underlining if possible, as students' eyes glance right over italics, and underlining is often associated with a title.

Following are characteristics to consider when writing the distracters (Davidson, 2011; Gareis & Grant, 2008; Little et al., 2012; Stiggins et al., 2004).

- **Provide one, and only one, correct answer:** For example, if one choice is ½ and another ³⁄₆ and there was not an explicit statement calling for the reduced form of fractions, then both answers are acceptable. In addition, if there are similar terms for a concept and both are used, students might miss the item, not because they don't know the concept but because the vocabulary is unfamiliar.

Older students tend to overthink these items, so providing space for students to explain their choice will lead to better information about student's understanding. If the explanation works, students should receive full credit.

- **Include plausible options that demonstrate a student's level of understanding:** To gather quality distracters, ask the question as a short answer and then use the incorrect student responses on later assessments as distracters. Jen L. Little and colleagues (2012) study the extent to which multiple-choice items could push students beyond mere retrieval of information to understanding that would last beyond the test itself. They suggest that this is possible if distracters are crafted carefully and misunderstanding is revealed to students as they determine why the key is right and the distracters are wrong. For example, when assessing *inference*, consider the following distracters—

  - An actual fact from the text

  - An opinion that might be generated from the text

  - A loose connection to the text's topic

- **Maintain a homogeneous feel in style, length, and visual display:** If one distracter begins with a verb, make them all begin with a verb. If one distracter is shorter than another, make another equally short so there is balance. If one distracter is a fraction and another a decimal, make two of them decimals and two fractions.

- **Keep distracters as brief and succinct as possible:** Place the bulk of the text in the stem.

- **Vertically stack the distracters and the key when possible:** Although it uses more paper and is not environmentally friendly, students are better able to compare possible choices when they are vertical versus horizontally organized on the page. Use ample white space.

- **Use capital letters for the key and distracters:** This originated with students transferring matching answers to bubble sheets. Lowercase letters take younger learners as well as students for whom English is a second language a few seconds longer to decipher.

- **Limit or eliminate the use of "all" or "none of the above":** They are too often used as the right answer. If you do use them, be sure that sometimes they are the correct answer and other times they are not.

- **Put the distracters (and the key) in a logical (alphabetical, short to long, numerical) order:** This reduces the time it takes for students to decipher and compare them. Often the first thing our brain does is to put lists in some type of order or look for a pattern. This eliminates that step.

- **Make sure distracters don't give away the answer:** Sometimes the distracters are so obscure and random that it is obvious they are incorrect. As a result, students choose the right answer not because they know the concept but because it is clear the other distracters don't make sense. Be sure students are not able to choose a response without knowing something beyond what is in the stem.

- **Check grammar, punctuation, and spelling:** Ensure everything is correct and consistent.

Deeper Cognitive-Level Considerations

Multiple-choice items can offer information about high-cognitive-level learning goals when written carefully. The following characteristics can offer insight into how to write higher-level multiple-choice items.

- **Set up a scenario and ask multiple questions that build on each other:** For example, pull a part of the text or a quote and ask students to select the choice that best reflects the meaning of the excerpt. Then, offer another question that asks which of the following sentences (choices are directly from the text) supports what they chose in question one. Assessment items posted on the Smarter Balanced (www.smarterbalanced.org/sample-items-and-performance-tasks) and PARCC (www.parcconline.org/samples/item-task-prototypes) websites provide excellent models from which to learn.

- **Provide data, graphs, pictures, cartoons, and diagrams, and then ask questions that require analysis or application:** Be sure to include distracters that represent possible misconceptions or surface-level interpretations.

- **Make sure the content and verb in the question match or exceed the level the standard requires:** For example, the question, Who wrote the Magna Carta? is basic recall, while asking, "Which item best represents the purpose of the Magna Carta?" also involves recall but has a little more depth.

- **Focus on complexity rather than difficulty:** The most a multiple-choice item can do is call for students to evaluate and select from a list of options. Asking students to explain their choice can also add depth to the item.

A Reading Example

The following example indicates a slightly higher-level question in that students must tease out the main idea and then support it with explanations using evidence from the text. In the question, shown in figure 4.8 written by a fifth-grade team in Owatonna, Minnesota, each distracter signals a potential misconception that could be used by the students to analyze their mistakes and by the teacher to provide effective instruction.

---

1. What is the main idea the author wants the reader to understand?

    a. Feral dogs are generally dangerous. (An isolated fact)

    b. Diclofenac given to livestock is killing vultures. (Contributes to the problem)

    c. The extinction of vultures is not good for humans. (Correct answer: main idea supported by a, b, and d)

    d. Vultures are an important part of the Parsi burial ritual. (Support for why extinction is not good)

2. What evidence from the text supports your answer?

Source: Amy Roberts and Elizabeth Zeman, Owatonna Schools, Minnesota. Used with permission.

Figure 4.8: Distracters containing misconceptions.

Again, use the template in figure 4.7 (page 62) to guide your multiple-choice item design. You may also select some multiple-choice questions for students to explain. To expedite scoring these items, students can fill in a response sheet like the one in figure 4.9 (page 66).

Provide an explanation of the following items. You need to describe your response only for the items listed in column one.		
Item	**Your Explanation**	**Scoring = 3 Points Possible**
12		• The explanation is convincing and well-supported. • The explanation is plausible. • The explanation uses clear language and sentence structure.
13		• The explanation is convincing and well-supported. • The explanation is plausible. • The explanation uses clear language and sentence structure.
14		• The explanation is convincing and well-supported. • The explanation is plausible. • The explanation uses clear language and sentence structure.

Figure 4.9: Sample response sheet.

Current Assessment Considerations for Cognitive Level

After a morning considering quality assessment practices, a veteran team of English teachers met for an hour and a half and went through their exam, identifying the learning goals behind each item. They were surprised to find that the assessment they designed did not reflect the cognitive level they had assumed was present. This simple assessment of their assessment led to a few revisions in the test that made it significantly better.

Where assessments already exist, it often makes sense to look at their cognitive level and revise them to better reflect the learning goals identified. The protocol in figure 4.10 guides an individual or team of teachers through this process.

Step 1. Identify the cognitive level of each item on the assessment, and place the item number in the third column of the table. Use the descriptions here or create your own. Cognitive level 1 (recollection, recognition, identification, computation) Cognitive level 2 (application, analysis, connection) Cognitive level 3 (evaluation, synthesis, argumentative literacy) **Step 2. In the second column, write the learning goal that corresponds with the item.** When interrogating items, look at the question and describe the learning goal that is being assessed. Pay close attention to the verb in the question. When identifying the cognitive level and learning goal, be sure

to phrase the learning goal with a verb and then a description, as shown in the following. (As a self-test, cover the learning goal, and see how close you come to stating it the same way.)

Step 3. Add up the total number of points or items in each cognitive level in the fourth column.

This step is designed to look at the percentage of importance (sometimes shown through the number of points that an item is worth) or the number of items focused at each cognitive level. Sometimes, our assessments do not reflect the required rigor or cognitive level we want our students to achieve. If too many items or points are located at the lower cognitive levels, this column will help us see that imbalance, and then we will be able to revise the assessment to better reflect the intended standards and cognitive level, or rigor.

Step 4. Comment on what you notice about the proportion of the assessment that falls in each cognitive level in the fifth column.

Then, make revisions to better represent the standards as well as what students are expected to learn. In addition, consider the criteria for rigor and relevance. Where in the assessment and in what ways are these appropriately applied?

Cognitive Level	Learning Goals and Topics	Item Numbers	Total Points	Your Thoughts and Revisions
Level 1	I can identify qualities of characters in literary text.	Item 1*	2	I will need to add another couple of questions at this level to see if students understand the gist of the text.
Level 2	I can analyze the main idea of a text.	Item 2*	4	This is a solid question, and I will be able to see their thinking and how they support their responses from the text they cite.
Level 3	I can summarize text. I can use evidence from the text to support my argument. I can compare and contrast key messages in multiple texts on the same topic.	Item 3*	20	They may write a draft of this essay and then revise it for the summative assessment.

Refer to sample items in figure 4.11 (page 68).

Figure 4.10: Protocol for revising cognitive level of assessment to reflect learning goals.

Figure 4.11 (page 68) shows sample items from the American dream assessment and their corresponding learning goals.

Item	Learning Goal

1. Which of the following best describes the main character, Dexter, in "Winter Dreams"?
 	
   A. Dreamy
 	
   B. Determined
 	
   C. Angry
 	
   D. Caring
	I can identify qualities of characters in literary text.

2. Which of the following statements best describes the main idea of the text?
 	
   A. Money doesn't buy happiness.
 	
   B. Determination is the way to achieve your dreams.
 	
   C. Relationships with the wrong people can squelch a dream.
 	
   D. Dreams desired may bring with them unexpected consequences.
 	
Explain why you think so, and use evidence from the story to support your opinion.
	I can analyze the main idea of a text.

3. We have been exploring the following question: How has the American dream changed over time? We have read "I Hear America Singing," by Walt Whitman (1860), and "Winter Dreams," by F. Scott Fitzgerald (1926). We have also read a survey on the American dream (Center for the Study of the American Dream, 2014). For this task, read "Dreaming America," by Joyce Carol Oates (1973) and view the NBC news clip describing and questioning the state of the American dream (Linn, 2013). Given the information in the article and the video, describe the key messages and how they develop. Explain your thinking using evidence from the text and video. In addition, compare and contrast the two pieces, again using evidence to support your thinking.	I can summarize text. I can use evidence from the text to support my argument. I can compare and contrast key messages in multiple texts on the same topic.

Figure 4.11: Sample items with corresponding learning goals.

Culturally Relevant Assessment Considerations

In *Motivating Students: 25 Strategies to Light the Fire of Engagement* (2011), Carolyn Chapman and I describe culturally relevant teaching based on the work of Geneva Gay. Gay (2002) describes the importance when designing curriculum of three components that are applicable to item design as well.

1. **Design a culturally relevant curriculum:** In assessment design, consider multicultural examples, facts, people, images, and situations. Move beyond stereotypes and tap into literature and stories of everyday citizens to construct items and tasks. As you create engaging tasks that are culturally relevant, also consider the strengths of the culture as well as the hot topics that generate lots of emotion.

2. **Enact a culturally diverse curriculum flexibly and responsively:** Tap into students to learn more about their interests, passions, and culture.

3. **Learn about cultural communication patterns:** There are many occasions during assessment design when we must tap into students' written and verbal communication to understand where they are in their achievement. By looking purposefully at students' communication patterns, we can ensure that they have all the information they need about the

methods we are using to assess their learning. In addition, we can ensure that the vocabulary used is familiar and understood; a lack of understanding of vocabulary is one of the biggest sources of error we encounter in our assessments.

See page 129 in the appendix for additional culturally relevant resources.

Special Needs Assessment Considerations

Julia, my niece, has a very rare genetic condition called Filippi Syndrome. She is an incredible child with gifts that range from being able to hum a tune in near perfect pitch (including Taylor Swift's *I Knew You Were Trouble* [Swift, Martin, & Shellback, 2012]) to finding resources on YouTube with ease and confidence. One of her teachers in early elementary school was determined to find some communication method that would allow Julia to communicate what she was thinking and feeling. She said, "We know there are many thoughts going on in her head. We just have to figure out the best way to help her get them out." Relentlessly, her teacher tried new avenues. From sign language to the iPad, there were many options. For Julia, the key to progress was to combine reading with pictures. One day, her teacher made a video of Julia reading this way and sent it to her mother. Receiving these snapshots was an incredible gift that built confidence and hope, both in Julia and in her family.

Of key importance when considering special needs is flexibility and providing multiple ways for students to demonstrate, communicate, and engage in their learning. John Savlia, James Ysseldyke, and Sara Bolt (2007) describe the challenge of classroom assessment and special education.

> Disability can pose a serious challenge to learning and to fully demonstrating knowledge and abilities. It is important for teachers to remember that the purpose of any form of CA [classroom assessment] is to assess the student's ability level instead of the effect of the disability condition. (Savlia et al., 2007, as cited in Xu, p. 442)

While students with special needs have individualized education programs that describe goals and the ways students will meet those goals, classroom assessment also needs to be flexible enough so that all students can engage and demonstrate learning. For example, assessments that require writing to show analysis, recall, or explanations may allow for students to audiotape or discuss their responses with another adult or peer. When assessments are focused on learning goals, teachers may select multiple methods that show understanding. The overall goal of assessment is to gather information about student learning to help students grow. Exercising flexibility in method and process can empower students to achieve more.

Understanding the strengths of a child and finding the best way to tap into those strengths is essential when considering the best methods for assessing students with diverse learning needs. Knowing the challenges students face and working in partnership with special education teachers allows for appropriate accommodations, resulting in assessments and tasks that best describe these students' achievement. See page 129 in the appendix for additional special needs resources.

English-as-a-Second-Language Assessment Considerations

When English is not a student's first language, assessment practice, both in design and use, must provide quality information that empowers students to learn more and does not shut them down. Hinok Yacob (2009) is a senior in an English learner college-essay writing class. He eloquently describes the need for students to feel confident and to understand that not knowing a language does not make one unimportant or stupid. He also advocates for teachers taking the opportunity to see diversity in background and language as strengths: "Students must be taught to hold their own voices and to ignore the teachers who have made them feel that what they've said is wrong, or bad or stupid. Teachers have chances to assert that students' backgrounds and language are unique and important" (Yacob, 2009, p. 4). There are many considerations when thinking about assessment for students for whom English is a second language. Some students are more fluent in their primary language than others. Some students have more experience and fluency with English than others. No one strategy or set of criteria will work for all. Knowing who your students are and ensuring that they can engage in the assessment is key.

One of the biggest considerations in your assessment practice is academic vocabulary. Consider giving support in the form of vocabulary translated into your students' first language. Some students may understand the concepts but not the way they are rendered in the English language. Unfortunately, non-native English speakers who are struggling with vocabulary are many times seen as language *deficient*, not language *different*, and are skipped over in terms of their linguistic needs. Find ways to give an academic vocabulary score along with a score on concepts. This results in more accurate feedback. Being flexible on the method and paying attention to the language of an assessment should not mean lowering expectations or cognitive level. See page 129 in the appendix for additional resources.

The Time Crunch

More complex, rigorous tasks are often not as easy to score as multiple-choice items. Following are a few thoughts on the logistics of creating such tasks without draining a teacher's time after school.

- **Have students use the final-exam time frame as a self-reflection time:** Students have written drafts of essays, problems, or tasks prior to the exam. They have also revised using feedback or minilessons prior to the exam. Students can now review their final exam (essay or test) and consider their strengths and challenges.

- **Ask students to produce drafts of a final task one to two weeks prior to the end of the unit or course:** Give them focused feedback on a few areas they need to revise and improve. Having this assignment due a few days prior to the end of the course gives teachers a few more days to review them.

- **Use a scoring checklist:** Easily check things off as opposed to writing out comments. The checklist contains the expectations, so the students are still able to see their strengths and next steps.

- **Craft rubrics and scoring guides that clearly outline the descriptions of learning:** This also speeds up the scoring process and allows for teachers to calibrate their scoring.

Develop Student Documents and Gather Necessary Materials

The second step of phase four is to lay out the test, rubric, or performance assessment you have designed and gather the materials that you will provide to the students. To be sure that they clearly understand the learning goal, task, and scoring criteria, consider the following.

- Provide clear and succinct directions.

- Gather materials or give access to technology and other resources that are required to engage in the assessment. Be sure financial resources and access to technology don't become barriers or requirements to do well.

- Use a visual layout that will result in students achieving more. Simple white space versus small and dense text is more open and inviting.

- Be careful not to make filling out a form or a graphic the end result. Any outline or visual organizer should be focused on the quality of information, more than on completing the boxes. Criteria can be brainstormed with students to ensure they understand that quality, not quantity, is the goal.

- Provide enough space for students to draw, write, or work solutions on the actual document if needed.

- If needed, create instructions for how much help teachers offer students or how the assessment should be administered.

When considering how to develop the student document for the second-grade money assessment, the team used a table to best organize where students will identify coins and show values. They made sure there was ample white space for students to work the problem and explain their thinking. Figure 4.12 shows the document that emerged from this planning and assessment design.

The ideas in this chapter are intended to help teachers create more valid and reliable assessments. In addition, the tips and templates are designed to promote more rigorous, relevant, and meaningful assessment tasks. When students are engaging in these types of high-quality assessments, they feel great pride in their work and want to spend time putting it forward.

In the next chapter, we will look at student investment in this process. However, the tips and tools in this chapter are also great to share with students as ways of creating classrooms centered on learning. Learners may find creating the actual items, tasks, and rubrics a meaningful experience; teachers and students working in partnership to create assessments can also be an experience that is rich and meaningful.

Put Phase Four Into Play

Phase four is where the planning and the task, item, and rubric design come together to create the actual documents that teachers share with students to demonstrate their learning. The second-grade money assessment shown in figure 4.12 depicts the document that students receive. (Visit **go.solution-tree.com /assessment** to listen to a screencast of Nicole modeling phase four for a fifth-grade reading assessment.)

Knowing the value of money and how to add and subtract money helps me make smart choices about how to spend and save.

Name: _____

Date: _____

Learning Goals

- I can critique another mathematician's solution.
- I can construct an argument supporting the process I used to solve the problem.
- I can make a model for my solution.
- I can use what I know about coins to solve real-world problems.
- I can add money.
- I can identify coins and their values.

Figure 4.12: Second-grade money-assessment plan.

Continued on next page →

Part 1: I can identify coins and their values. _____ 8 points (1 point each)

Write the value of each coin pictured. Use the word bank to write the name of each coin.

Coin	What's the *value* of the coin?	What's the *name* of the coin?

Word Bank

Penny	Dime
Nickel	Quarter

Part 2: I can add money. _____ 12 points (3 points each)

Grab, Draw, and Add: Gently *grab* the coins from the bag, *draw* the coins, and *add* the total. Do this four times.

Sample	5¢ 5¢ 1¢ 25¢	36¢
1.		
2.		
3.		
4.		

Part 3: I can use what I know about coins to solve real-world problems.

  I can make a model for my solution.

  I can construct an argument supporting the process I used to solve the problem.

We have been studying money and the best ways to solve problems and represent solutions. Provide a solution and explanation for the following problems:

Sara loves chocolate. The candy bar costs 25 cents. Her friend, Tasha, loves Skittles. A bag costs 35 cents.

How much money will it cost for the two treats?

_____

If Sara and Tasha wanted to have candy three days in a row, how much money would they need?

_____

Draw the coins you would use to pay for these treats. Name the amounts inside the circle as in the following examples.

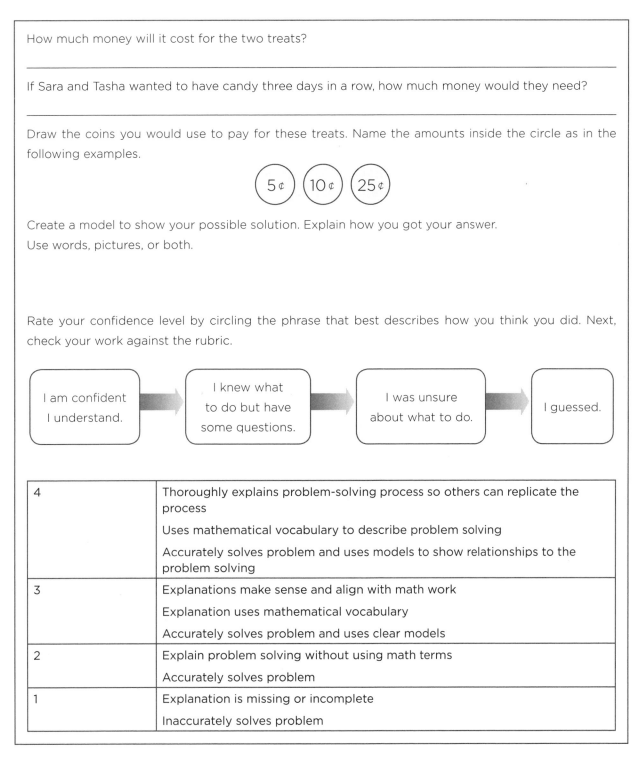

Create a model to show your possible solution. Explain how you got your answer.
Use words, pictures, or both.

Rate your confidence level by circling the phrase that best describes how you think you did. Next, check your work against the rubric.

| I am confident I understand. | → | I knew what to do but have some questions. | → | I was unsure about what to do. | → | I guessed. |

4	Thoroughly explains problem-solving process so others can replicate the process
	Uses mathematical vocabulary to describe problem solving
	Accurately solves problem and uses models to show relationships to the problem solving
3	Explanations make sense and align with math work
	Explanation uses mathematical vocabulary
	Accurately solves problem and uses clear models
2	Explain problem solving without using math terms
	Accurately solves problem
1	Explanation is missing or incomplete
	Inaccurately solves problem

Continued on next page →

Part 4: I can critique another mathematician's solution. *This is completed after all students have completed part 3.*

Your Name: _____

Mathematician's Name: _____

Provide this mathematician with some feedback on his or her solution to part 3 using the following questions:

1. What part of the solution makes sense and is done well?

2. What questions do you have for the mathematician?

3. What advice might you offer this mathematician?

Criteria

_____ I provided specific statements about his or her solution.

_____ I gave examples from his or her work explaining my statement.

_____ I provided an accurate reflection on his or her work.

Visit **go.solution-tree.com/assessment** for a blank reproducible form of this figure.

Pause and Ponder

The following questions are designed to help individual teachers or teams focus on the essential ideas presented in this chapter.

- What is rigor? What characteristics make an assessment rigorous? Consider making a list of these characteristics and using it to reflect on and revise a current assessment.

- What is relevance? What characteristics make an assessment relevant? Consider making a list of these characteristics and using it to reflect on and revise a current assessment.

- How would you describe the three key elements to effectively designing an item or a task?

- Which cognitive framework best informs your work in designing items and tasks?

- What process or protocol might be most useful in considering designing, critiquing, and revising your assessments? Consider developing your own protocol using some of the key ideas in this chapter.

- What is the best use of rubrics? How could they help students learn more? How could they help students understand the learning goals more clearly? Are there rubrics already created in your school or system that can be used or revised to inform your assessment work?

Determining Student Investment and the Reporting Method

A great teacher of mine was my tenth-grade English teacher. . . . What I remember and miss dearly about being his student was the effort he put into reminding us to slow down and think and reflect—think and reflect about what we read and about what we are doing. This wasn't just a technique I learned to incorporate in school; it was a technique I was able to carry inside of me and apply to my life.

—Hinok Yacob, High School Senior

Communicating and using assessment information are among the most powerful ways to build student investment and create a classroom culture focused on learning. Hinok talks about the power of reflection and slowing down. He learned this through the actions and interactions with his teacher, who intentionally structured this type of reflection so learning would become transparent to the student. This is the kind of reflection on which student investment is built. In *Visible Learning: A Synthesis of Over 800 Meta-Analyses Relating to Achievement*, Hattie (2009) describes a key pattern from his synthesis of over 800 meta-analyses of a comprehensive list of educational practices. Central to this finding is the importance of the role students play in their learning.

> It is also what learners *do* that matters. So often learners become passive recipients of teachers' lessons, but . . . the aim is to make students active in the learning process—through action by teachers and others—until the students reach the stage where they become their own teachers, they can seek out optimal ways to learn new material and ideas, they can seek resources to help them in this learning, and when they can, set appropriate and more challenging goals. Students need to be involved in determining success criteria, setting higher expectations, and being open to experiences relating to differing ways of knowing and problem solving. (p. 37)

In phase five of Design in Five, teachers intentionally plan for students to invest, which involves various ways learners act on information to grow and improve and come to see their assessment score or mark in terms of learning. In order for students to do this kind of reflection, assessments must communicate specific information about students' learning, and that is the first step in phase five—creating a scoring scheme. Whether formative or summative, the way information is used by teachers and students is more effective with better, more descriptive scoring schemes. These schemes are the foundation of better grading and reporting practices.

Waiting for the "grade" can be both exhilarating and dreadful, depending on past experience and current expectations of teachers and families. Grading is emotional for both the evaluator and the evaluated. Both teachers and students want to be affirmed, to feel valued and competent. Grades and marks are often the most frequent way teachers and schools communicate, report, and monitor progress for individual students, but grades also have the potential to shut down learning and undermine confidence and hope. The purpose of a grade or a mark is to communicate learning (Guskey, 2005; O'Connor, 2002). But often so many factors other than learning influence a single grade or a final mark. In fact, students rarely connect grades to their learning. For that matter, they rarely connect their homework, instructional activities, or what they are doing and producing through homework and instructional activities to what they are learning. A quality assessment communicates information about the learning that was intended to be assessed, not just an overall score, percentage, or symbol. In phase five, teachers plan how to best communicate the learning students have achieved and the next steps that will help them improve. Phase five has two steps.

1. Create a scoring scheme that reflects the learning.

2. Choose strategies to foster student investment.

Create a Scoring Scheme That Reflects the Learning

When asked about the meaning of grades, one high school student sums up the most common response: "A grade? A grade doesn't reflect my learning or what I know. It has everything to do with how hard you try and how much homework you hand in." The research on grading describes the meaning of grades as muddy and complex. One set of scores or body of evidence can yield many different interpretations, depending on how it is calculated, weighted, or configured (Guskey, 2002, 2011; Marzano, 2006, 2010; O'Connor, 2002, 2007; Reeves, 2011). In truth, any symbol, even a smiley face or a check mark, can be just as confusing and not clearly communicate to even our youngest students what they are learning.

In this step of phase five, teachers intentionally plan scoring schemes that provide students information about their strengths and weaknesses in terms of learning goals and criteria. Specific information about the learning that is achieved and the next steps for growth provides hope and possibility for improvement and clearer communication about learning (Brophy, 2004; Hattie & Timperley, 2007). With better information about learning, the assessment can be used formatively by teachers to design instruction that meets students' needs and by students to learn from their mistakes through revision or analyzing and fixing errors. In the case of students who performed well, tying marks to learning is one step toward reshaping how students see their grades—moving away from seeing the grade as evaluation of their personal worth toward seeing it as a description of their achievement. When asked how to improve their grade, teachers can point students to something tangible and meaningful—a learning goal that needs more attention.

When assessment information is used summatively, giving students more information about what that grade or score means in terms of learning helps them connect their work, their assessments, and their grades to what they are achieving.

Types of Scoring Schemes

When communicating the score of an assessment to students, include scores on the individual criteria or learning goals as well as an overall mark or percentage. Some teachers put the learning goals right on the assessment, so students begin to see these connections. Others link percentages, grades, or items directly to the learning goals. As students receive their assessments back, they may be also asked to self-assess (step two of phase five) as long as they know which items or tasks go with which learning goal. When students can see their work in terms of learning goals, they can refocus and self-regulate their work, based on how they did on the test, paper, or dialogue.

In some standards-based systems, practices have moved away from points and grades and now use symbols or descriptors, such as "beginning standard," "approaching standard," "meeting standard," or "exceeding standard," to describe varying levels of achievement on a report card. Scores on individual assessments can also be reported with this same standards-based marking system. This means that items are written to align to the type of work students must achieve at each level.

In the second-grade money assessment, there are assessment items for each learning goal, as shown in figure 5.1 (page 78), and students receive a score for each learning goal. The rating scale matches students' standards-based marks, and they achieve at various levels based on how they solved the problem tied to that particular standard. The second-grade money assessment is scored in four parts. In the first two sections, students receive points based on whether their responses are either right or wrong. Students must achieve 80 percent of the points to show proficiency. Visit **go.solution-tree.com/assessment** to download a copy of the second-grade scoring scheme and other examples.

- **Part 1:** I can identify coins and their values. _____ (8 points)
- **Part 2:** I can use what I know about coins to add money. _____ (12 points; 3 points each)

Students will get their score on a rubric for part 3. The problem has more than one way to get to a solution and varying proficiency levels for modeling and explaining thinking. In a standards-based grading situation, the rubric would mirror the scoring scheme on the report card.

- **Part 3:** I can use what I know about coins to solve real-world problems. I can make a model for my solution. (rubric)
- **Part 4:** I can critique another mathematician's solution. (scoring checklist)

The geometry test in figure 5.2 (page 78) also communicates items and scores by learning goal (or, using this high school's terminology, by performance indicator). Students track their achievement based on performance indicators and can easily use that information to identify strengths and next steps. The teacher scores each learning goal as a 1 (beginning standard), 2 (approaching standard), 3 (meeting standard), or 4 (exceeding standard). Visit **go.solution-tree.com/assessment** for another sample geometry assessment using rubrics.

Score	Learning Goals	Items on Assessment	Student Score
4 Exceeding Standard	I can critique another mathematician's solution.	Part 4: Scoring checklist	
3 Meeting Standard	I can make a model for my solution. I can use what I know about coins to solve real-world problems. I can use what I know about coins to add money.	Part 3: Rubric Part 2: 12 points; 3 points each	
2 Approaching Standard	I can identify coins and their values.	Part 1: 8 points	
1 Beginning Standard	I can complete the assessment with guidance from the teacher or another adult.		

Figure 5.1: Second-grade money assessment standards-based scoring scheme.

Name: _____

Unit 4 Test: Polygon Properties

Performance Indicator	Questions Assessed	Assessment			
Classify polygons by their sides and angles.	1, 2, 3, 4, 6	1	2	3	4
Use relationships between the interior and exterior angles of polygons to solve problems.	5, 6, 8, 13	1	2	3	4
Use the properties of parallelograms, kits, and trapezoids to solve problems.	7, 9, 19, 11	1	2	3	4
Use midsegment properties of triangles and trapezoids to solve problems.	10, 12	1	2	3	4
Use properties of special quadrilaterals of polygons.	14, 15, 16, 17	1	2	3	4
Write deductive arguments using properties of polygons.	18	1	2	3	4
Demonstrate understanding of slope and y-intercepts in graphing linear equations.	14	1	2	3	4
Demonstrate precision.	All	1	2	3	4

Source: Monica Carter, Karen Needler, & Peter Booth, Champlain Valley Union High School, Hinesburg, Vermont. Used with permission.

Figure 5.2: Percentages linked to learning goals on a geometry test.

Rubric Scoring

Rubrics are intended to provide more information to students about the quality of their work. As a result, turning a rubric score into a grade seems counterintuitive. However, there are times when we do this because we need to quantify achievement at that moment in time. Robert J. Marzano (2010), offers a conversion scale shown in table 5.1 that is helpful when turning a rubric score into a percentage. However, the best use of a rubric is to describe learning and assign a more standards-based mark.

Table 5.1: Converting Rubric Scores to Percentage Scores

Scale or Rubric Score	Percentage Score
4	100
3.5	95
3.0	90
2.5	80
2.0	70
1.5	65
1.0	60
Below 1.0	50

Another way to consider a conversion scale is to consider the following, where an A is the top of a level 3, meaning students have mastered the required standards. A high *A* is obtained by demonstrating deeper work. The argument for a higher grade isn't about getting more points but about producing higher-quality work. Proficiency is set at 80 percent. Students not achieving get a *not yet*, so they cannot settle for a score, be let off the hook, or lose hope because of the low score that digs them into a hole too deep to escape from (see table 5.2).

Table 5.2: Alternate Conversion Scale

Scale or Rubric Score	Percentage Score
4	94–100
3	80–93
2	70–79
1	Not Yet

Step one in phase five, creating scoring schemes, is about creating tables or descriptions that give students better information about what their individual assessments mean. These tables are given to students along with their assessment. This is a critical aspect of setting up high-quality grading and reporting practices that better reflect a student's overall performance, including achievement of standards and work habits that are necessary for success in school and life. The next section offers a brief dialogue on systemic policies and practices to improve grading practices. For a deeper study and implementation of high-quality grading practices, consult Douglas Reeves's (2011) *Elements of Grading: A Guide to Effective Practice*, Ken O'Connor's

(2002, 2011) *How to Grade for Learning* and *A Repair Kit for Grading: 15 Fixes for Broken Grades* (2nd ed.), Tom Guskey and Jane Bailey's (2010) *Developing Standards-Based Report Cards*, and Tom Guskey's (2015) *On Your Mark: Challenging the Conventions of Grading and Reporting*.

Better Grading Practices

In the spirit of moving to grades and reporting systems that communicate more effectively, we must start to create policies and practices that move away from students arguing for a point or two of extra credit just to improve their grades. Instead of asking questions like, "How much is this worth? Is this graded?" students would begin to consider questions such as, "How do I revise this work or fix mistakes to learn more? How can I demonstrate deeper understanding to improve my grade?" In creating a culture of learning, we want students to understand that their grades will improve if they revise, improve, and submit quality work. Marzano (2010) discusses student-generated assessment as one example of this phenomenon; in student-generated assessment, students who are crystal clear on the learning goals and their level of proficiency begin to bring evidence of improved proficiency to the teacher. Student investment strategies such as descriptive feedback practices and student self-assessment structures communicate a focus on learning. To further consider how to move our grading practices forward in ways that help students learn and invest, it is important to consider how some grading practices influence motivation.

We often use grades as a mechanism to motivate students. Teachers lament, "If I don't grade it, students won't do it." But do grades really motivate students? They do seem to motivate some students who are successful and have a clear idea of what they want to do in the future (Hattie & Timperley, 2007; McMillan, 2013). One student states, "I'm happy with myself when I get good grades . . . I wanted to make myself better." Some of my students would make compelling arguments to increase their grade from 95 to 98. But consider what happens when these same students who have a track record of success make a mistake. They often are devastated. In the absence of any other description of a grade's meaning, students often see it as a reflection of their self-worth (Hattie & Timperley, 2007). In this context, grades do not represent learning.

For those students who are not successful or who have repeatedly failed, grades do not motivate. Rather, they consistently break down confidence and hope (Hattie, 2009; Reeves, 2011). In *Elements of Grading*, Reeves (2011) challenges teachers to test the theory that grades motivate students to achieve more: he invites them to make a list of all the students who received zeroes on assignments at the end of quarter one. Then he asks them to make another list of all the students who received zeroes on assignments at the end of quarter two. If grades, or in this case zeroes, motivate students to turn in their work, the two lists should be different. More often than not, students who are not achieving during quarter one are also not achieving in quarter two. In this scenario, grades are not the motivating factor. There are other factors at play, and a different strategy to get students to engage in the work must be created. For example, is the student demonstrating understanding of the concept but just not handing in the homework? Is the student overwhelmed with homework and confused about how to start? Is the student so busy with after school activities or babysitting younger siblings that they are too exhausted to do the work? The answer to *why* students are not completing their work determines the best course of action.

Motivation for student learning and academic achievement is multifaceted. The research on motivation suggests that students are motivated when they feel confident that their effort and hard work will equate to success in both their grades and their learning (Martin, 2008). High school senior Gertrude Mongare (2009) describes the moment a teacher changed the course of her schooling by using the occasion of a poor grade on a summative test to have a conversation:

> She suddenly looked up smiling and said, "Hey kiddo, I knew you would come in today. Have a seat and I'll be right with you." I was surprised she was not mad at me. I pricked myself with my pencil to clarify that it was no dream. My heart stopped racing and I took out my test while I waited for her. She was soon done and in no time she came and sat next to me. She then said, "I have noticed that you are struggling as per your test, is there anything that may have led to this?" I looked at her and said no but she could tell I was a bit nervous. She looked at me and I could tell she knew there was something wrong. I do not remember how I opened up and started talking to her but it was after that afternoon that I got the courage to ask questions and go for after school tutoring.
>
> My math grade gradually improved and by the time the semester grades were sent home, I had tremendously improved. The techniques she showed me to improve my math helped me improve my grades in other classes that I struggled with. She helped me improve my study skills, test taking strategies and most importantly improving my relationships with other teachers. (p. 3)

This event illustrates the power of using assessment well to deepen achievement and engagement. If the poor grade had not been addressed or the teacher had not said, "Come and see me," this opportunity to grow would have been lost. In this case, a low grade prompted the teacher to start a conversation that led to the root cause of Gertrude's low achievement. That one conversation led to the student's higher achievement and greater feelings of confidence. Gertrude was able to more independently invest in her learning from that point forward. It's all about the *use* of these scores.

In contrast, some research suggests that putting a grade or percentage on a piece of work to help the student improve is not the most effective strategy, because students often dismiss any comments and focus on the grade (Butler, 1988; Hattie, 2009). In fact, it can distract from any comment or focus that might promote learning. Ruth Butler (1988) finds that students' learning increased on average by 30 percent when receiving only comments. When receiving only grades or grades and descriptive comments, students showed no gain in achievement. This suggests that if we want students to learn from comments, we may need to delay the grade and require revision. If comments are intended to promote learning, students must revise their work based on the comment. With a grade and a comment and only an invitation to revise, students will often just look at the grade. Those who really need to revise won't accept the invitation. If students are going to do the work even when it is not graded, teachers must plan and require that students use those comments to improve their work and that can be part of a teacher's instructional or lesson plan. These comments that are required for revision should directly contribute to students getting better so they are well-prepared for the summative assessment or positioned to revise the task and bring it to a more final form. Later in the chapter, there are suggestions for effective and efficient feedback practices.

Specific Grading Practices to Consider

An overall reporting system (including marks, grades, feedback, and work habits) creates opportunities to communicate formatively. Students use what they learn from the assessment to identify strengths and take action to revise. A balanced reporting system also creates intentional opportunities (report cards, end of units, or themes) to communicate summatively, so students and families are getting clear information about progress towards achieving the grade-level standards and about work habits such as timeliness and perseverance. A system that incorporates both formative and summative communication, beyond just one symbol (a grade or standards-based mark) two to four times a year will begin to help students make these connections. Standards-based report cards are a way to communicate more effectively with students and families about their learning and their engagement. The report card in itself does not increase achievement.

Rather, the use of the higher-quality assessment information is what increases achievement. Report cards are a way to communicate more effectively and thus empower families and students to understand their strengths and areas of growth.

Design Proactive Strategies and Policies to Connect Increased Proficiency With Improved Grades

If students are able to complete work successfully without doing any of the practice provided, we must look at the challenge level of the learning goals being offered. This involves analyzing the standard so we can discern the simple to complex learning goals (phase two). All students need to meet a certain level of the standard. For those learners who come to us already knowing the standard, or who achieve quickly, our instruction needs to push their thinking and learning. Only then will the grade and the work be meaningful and relevant. A parent reflected that a lower grade is the only thing that got his child's attention and made him take stock of his behavior. He asked, "If a grade doesn't do that, what will?" But handing in an assignment so you can get a good grade doesn't teach responsibility or help students learn more—it teaches compliance. Compliance is important when tied to respect, but we also need to provide more meaningful challenges to students, so we are not policing work that doesn't support learning.

Retakes are a common practice that is both vehemently supported and abhorred. The argument in favor of retakes is that we do not want arbitrary time frames to limit learning. Some students need additional time to achieve the standard. Retake policies can provide that additional time for students to learn the most essential ideas. The grade in this case communicates the extent to which they learned—no matter what the time frame. In contrast, those who are frustrated with retakes lament the incredible amount of time spent on crafting multiple assessments and spending time administering retakes and meeting with students on prior learning as they move toward new learning and units.

Where should we spend our assessment energy? In a balanced and high-quality assessment practice, most of the time and energy are spent responding to formative information prior to a summative assessment. When students reach a point at which they are taking or submitting summative evidence, there should be no surprises. If a lot of students are failing or not achieving on the assessment, we may want to take a look at what's happening *prior* to the summative. Determine how many students are not achieving on the summative. If more than 20 percent are not proficient, review instructional practices. Did students need more practice? How could instruction be responsive to students' understanding, especially on essential standards? Covering it all won't raise achievement.

> *Where should we spend our assessment energy? In a balanced and high-quality assessment practice, most of it is spent responding to formative information prior to a summative assessment.*

Retaking is a very powerful practice, and an emphasis on retaking signals to students that we want all of them to achieve—that the learning we expect from students is essential and important enough to allow more time for them to get it. Some teachers observed that some students count on simply retaking the test if they don't do well. Even asking as the first test is given, when is the retake? A quick fix for this strategy is twofold: (1) students must fix their mistakes, and (2) they must practice before the retake. Students do not retake an assessment without evidence of work and deeper learning. Any student waiting for the retake will think twice the next time around after having to do more work before the second shot. The issue of who gets to do a retake is also important here. Teachers must determine what is proficient. If students are not proficient, they *must* retake—there is no invitation. This means that retakes must be built into the schedule. Some teachers build retakes into the unit map. Others use additional study or advisory time for retakes. In either case, it is not an option. This also means that the assessments students retake must be essential and incredibly meaningful.

Another issue that arises is how to score the retake. I advocate that the retake should replace the original score in its entirety. *If students get only a certain percentage of credit after a retake, it sends a message that how fast you learn it is more important than if you learn it.* Students often ask, "How much is this worth?" Without full credit, they may not work as hard. This also brings up the question of those students who are proficient but want a better grade. There is no right or wrong answer here. Allowing students to retake to get a better grade can be really motivating, but students must demonstrate a deeper understanding, not just get more answers correct. Some teachers will ask students to generate their own evidence to show they have a better understanding. It is not so much a retake in that case as it is another product that shows understanding. Getting to this type of practice starts to shift the focus to learning.

When reviewing or creating a retake policy, consider the following questions.

- Who does the retake?
- What assessments get retakes?
- What is the time frame for the retake?
- How will we review the retake policy? What will be the indicators that it is working? Not working?
- What are the qualitative data that will determine the policy's effectiveness? How do students describe the benefits of the retakes? Are they focused on learning or getting a better grade?
- What are the quantitative data that will determine the policy's effectiveness? How many students are retaking? How much time is spent on retaking (teachers and students)?

Report Work Habits Separately From Achievement

Many parents and families fear that if the work-habit aspects of school—such as taking responsibility for turning things in on time, coming to class on time, and putting work in the right format—are not factored into their grade, students won't learn them. When work comes in late, when students come in late, when students are disruptive in a discussion, a teacher's job becomes more difficult. Sometimes teachers attempt to use grades to try to change behavior. For some students, this will work, but for those who are compliant, already working hard, and being responsible, this strategy adds tremendous stress and pressure and creates a lot of work for the teacher. For those students who are late to class and late in handing in work, it often sinks them deeper into a hole that is hard to climb out of because they are consistently losing points. Teachers must constantly track who is getting work in on time and who is late, and they must have conversations with kids that focus on behavior. Reporting work habits and achievement separately can be as simple as putting two scores on the top of a paper—one for the quality or achievement of the work and another for its timeliness and neatness, or for other factors the teacher and student have agreed are important work habits.

Organize Grades by Learning Goal, Standard, or Task, Not by Assessment Method

Districts, schools, and classrooms need to be cautious when crafting policies that base percentage grades on particular assessment methods. When mandates require a certain percentage of a grade to be calculated based on homework, tests, projects, or daily work, good intentions can have unintended negative effects. In attempting to ensure that a grade is calculated mostly on summative assessments and recent events, for example, policies sometimes limit the weight of homework and increase the weight of summative assessments. But this can create more issues for teachers who are trying to motivate and engage students who are now hyper aware that homework and daily work are not worth as much as tests and projects. In addition, distributing percentages assumes that all teachers use these methods in similar ways. The communication with parents regarding the learning can also get muddled in the process. In short, it becomes more difficult to grade for learning when the percentages are based on method as opposed to being based on learning goal.

This difficulty is also true when establishing a policy about the percentages of formative and summative assessment that contributes to the overall grade. This policy moves closer to the goal of a grade reflecting achievement at a moment in time, because it requires that the majority of the evidence contributing to an overall grade comes after students have practiced a concept. Yet it still carries the potential for students to focus more on getting points and grades than on learning. For this policy to work effectively, there must be a very clear understanding that formative assessment is practice and that practice must be tied tightly to the summative evidence. If there is only a loose connection, students still see an event such as homework as formative, versus making revisions and fixing errors and getting better. Now, students will ask, "Is this formative or summative?" Again, the focus is not on learning but on gaining points, and savvy students will consider how much effort to put into something when the focus is still on the grade. This policy falls short, because there can be no alignment to what's practiced in formative assessment and how that now contributes to better performance on a summative assessment of the same standard. If the practice is tightly tied to learning, it should be evident that when students improve—not just when they hand in all their work—their grade improves. Anything can be formative or summative depending on how it is used.

The recording templates that follow show ways teachers have found to record scores so that it is easier to track progress and calculate a grade that better represents students' proficiency at the time of the report card. Whether standards based or traditional, recording scores in this way provides better information for students and teachers about the achievement of standards. Teachers also include a separate section for work habits.

Organize By Essential Standard. In this tracking mechanism, teachers record students' achievement according to essential standards. An example of scores recorded by essential standard in relationship to practice (F for formative) and proficiency (S for summative) is shown in figure 5.3. Each assessment can be scored using an overall percentage or grade. This requires that the points allocated on each assessment must be tied to the standard (something we planned in phase three, the assessment plan). In addition, if a school has moved to scoring schemes that are standards based such as the 4, 3, 2, 1 scoring system shown in table 5.2 (page 79), it can be recorded by rubric score. Scores can then be moved from formative (F) to summative (S), based on individual student performance. So, if a student mastered the content right away, demonstrated by a formative assessment, that evidence might be moved to the summative row for that student. Another student may have really struggled on that same formative assessment and so it remains formative, and that student will have the opportunity to learn more and then show evidence of that new understanding in another assessment. This form offers flexibility in the types of evidence used to calculate grades. In addition, each standard has a rubric that describes various levels of achievement. These rubrics are designed to reflect the cognitive levels of a ladder sketched out in phase two of Design in Five. This

Essential Standards		Hierarchy of Life — The learner will identify major organizational levels of life and be able to classify organisms. (Ch 1)			Scientific Inquiry — The learner will describe the nature of discovery science and hypothesis-based science. (Ch 2)			Methods of Studying Science — The learner will describe examples of studying behavior through observations and experiments. (Ch 3)				Chemistry in Living Things — The learner will identify macro-molecules and describe their importance in living things. (Ch 4)				Overall Quarter 1 Grade
Student A	F	50%	70%	50%	66%	54%	45%					45%				
	S			80%			90%	80%	80%	90%	100%		86%	92%	95%	90% (median)
Student B	F		60%		65%			45%			45%	45%				
	S	80%	80%	100%	80%	80%	96%		85%	97%			80%	96%	100%	90% (median)

Figure 5.3: Scores according to essential standard.

Visit **go.solution-tree.com/assessment** for a blank reproducible form of this figure.

means the scores represent assessments—formal and informal based on the rubrics designed for each standard.

Figure 5.3 also illustrates four of the eight essential standards in this course. The final column provides space to calculate the overall grade. Columns in each of the essential standards would be added to accommodate formative and summative assessment scores. This form is indicating that everything gets a grade—formative and summative, but the summative evidence is what is calculated into the final grade. In a model where formative assessment is not graded, the formative column would consist of descriptive comments, or rubric scores indicating to what extent the standard was achieved. The important aspect of this form is that students can always show evidence of achievement and that will count towards an overall score. In addition, these scores are not averaged; they are using other measures of central tendency—in this case, the median, to avoid the issue of scores skewed by individual really high or really low scores. Visit http://cvulearns.weebly.com for additional examples from Champlain Valley Union High School in Hinesburg, Vermont.

Organize by Standard and Task. In figure 5.4 (page 86) the reporting form reflects assessment information by standard and task. It's easy to see how students grow based on this form. Students are constantly improving their reading of informational text in key ideas and details. This model works well to document growth and proficiency within these goals—reading, writing, data analysis, problem solving, and argumentative literacy are among a few areas that work well in this context. At reporting periods, where teachers must mark report cards, these areas mirror the standards-based report card and the evidence that is most recent is used to score the report card. If teachers are using traditional grades, these scores could be percentages or points and then overall percentages are calculated based on the most recent scores or the median score in order to avoid really high scores or really low scores being too influential in reporting achievement at a moment in time for reporting purposes (O'Connor, 2002).

	Key Ideas and Details				Craft and Structure				Integration of Knowledge and Ideas			
	Task 1	Task 2	Task 3	Task 4	Task 1	Task 2	Task 3	Task 4	Task 1	Task 2	Task 3	Task 4
	9/16	9/18	9/23	9/25	9/30	10/2	10/7	10/9	10/14	10/16	10/21	10/23
Student Name												
Ali	2	3	3	4	3	3	4	4	3	4	3	3
Carlos	1	1	1	2	3	3	3	3	1	1	2	3
Jem	2	3	3	4	3	3	4	4	3	3	2	3

Figure 5.4: Scores according to standard and task.

Choose Strategies to Foster Student Investment

The second step in phase five is to craft a student-investment strategy. Student investment is the extent to which students are engaged in their learning and moving toward independence in describing where they are and how to grow. This takes time, and teachers should therefore regard the time students invest in wrestling with their learning strengths and next steps as part of instruction, as opposed to something additional they have to fit in. Student investment is another way in which we make learning the focus of our work.

When designing formative assessments for students who are invested, the strategies should focus on *how* students fix mistakes, revise their work, and actively engage in getting better. When designing summative assessments, the strategies should focus on self-assessment, goal setting, and attaching meaning to grades and scores. Where there is deep student investment, the culture of the school and classroom is focused on learning, and students use instruction and assessment to understand where they are in their learning. This information in turn leads to action, with students seeing value, relevance, and meaning in their work. In these spaces, students strive to thrive—they gain confidence and efficacy, because they are seeing results. As they gain confidence through understanding and feeling successful, students begin to learn how to learn—and to persevere when something is rough. Truthfully, students don't always get excited about revising their work, but as teachers require it and build it into instruction, students see results, and that in itself is engaging. Wiliam describes what he regards as the *only* 21st century skill.

> The model that says "learn while you're at school, while you're young, the skills that you will apply during lifetime" is no longer tenable. The skills that you can learn when you're at school will not be applicable. They will be obsolete by the time you get into the workplace and need them—except for one skill. The one really competitive skill is the skill of being able to learn. It is the skill of being able not to give the right answer to questions about what you were taught in school, but to make the right response to situations that are outside the scope of what you were taught in school. We need to produce people who know how to act when they're faced with situations for which they were not specifically prepared. (Wiliam, 2013)

Student questions—such as "Is this right?," "What do I do?," or "I don't know!"—take up incredible amounts of teacher time and energy. In a classroom in which students are invested, however, learners begin to trust their own judgment and do not rely solely on the teacher for affirmation or direction. With more confidence, students do better on complex tasks. When they come to something they don't know on a standardized test, they no longer freeze, guess, or skip over it.

When we work toward student investment, we create an environment in which students:

- **Have language to describe their learning**—"I can" statements are posted in classrooms, on assessments, on homework, on examples of student work, and on rubrics. Students use these displayed learning goals to reflect on instructional activities and assessments.

- **Have a clear idea of quality and not-so-quality work**—Students look at work and describe what's good, what needs work, and how to make it better or solve it more effectively.

- **Take action on descriptive feedback**—Students use comments from a teacher or a peer to improve or fix work.

- **Revise their work**—Students actively review their errors and fix their work or improve their writing or presentations.

- **Self-reflect on what the assessment means in terms of their learning**—Students use their assessments to identify strengths and next steps.

- **Set goals based on assessment information**—Students use the next steps from their self-reflection, and set a goal for improvement, describing how they will know when they have improved. This description often comes from a rubric or criteria. If students have scored a 2 on the rubric, they look to the 3 or 4 to set a goal to improve.

- **Make an action plan (in partnership with teachers) to achieve their goals and improve**—Teachers provide opportunities and require students to act on the plan—for example, students may fix mistakes on a quiz for homework or use feedback to revise during in-class instructional activities.

- **Share their work and plans to improve**—Through the simple act of students sharing their work and how they changed or plan to improve it, we hold them accountable to learning as opposed to compliance.

While these practices can lead to student investment, it is the interactions among peers and teachers and the responsiveness of the teacher toward student dialogue, questions, comments, and work that make student investment a reality and achievement increase (Chappuis, 2009; Hattie, 2009). In other words, each of these practices may lead to more student investment and a deeper culture of learning, but how they play out in different classrooms for different students must be part of the responsiveness a teacher practices. Specifically, teachers are paying attention to how students respond to different student-investment strategies. Teachers adjust based on student engagement and evidence of learning. This is the art of teaching.

Describing Learning

In order for students to stop or reduce the amount of time they spend comparing their grades or scores to those of others and focus on their learning, they need more information. When teachers provide quality and not-quality examples, students learn the language of what we want them to understand. Using the frame "I can . . ." or teaching students the language of the standards is one aspect of this work. But simply posting learning goals on the wall or on an assessment is only the beginning. This goes back to how we ask students to use these statements. Consider the take-a-stand example.

> I can use evidence to support an argument. This means I can use evidence from the text to back up my claim and explain how the text evidence supports the claim.
>
> How confident am I about this target?
>
> - I understand and can independently do this!
> - I have an idea about where to begin!
> - I'm confused and do not know what to do!

In figure 5.5, students see three learning goals at the top of the assessment. After reading an article and viewing a news clip multiple times, they construct an argument for or against the idea of paying for the costs of rescuing those who refused to evacuate during Hurricane Sandy, which devastated the East Coast of the United States in 2012. Students construct an essay, consult with peers, revise the essay, and then indicate their confidence level on each criterion. There is also a box for teachers to add their comments and score. The formative part of this assessment consists of the draft, feedback, and revisions; the summative part is the final draft scored by teachers.

Name: _____

Learning Goals:

- I can use the active voice to communicate a message.

- I can use the active voice to argue a point.

- I can use evidence from the text and other media sources to communicate a stance.

Take a Stand: Should Hurricane Sandy victims who did not evacuate pay for the cost of their rescue? Support your position with at least two reasons.

Criteria	Student Check	Teacher Comments
Includes a clear position	• I got it. • I have some questions. • I am unsure.	
Supports a position with specific examples from the text and clear explanations	• I got it. • I have some questions. • I am unsure.	
Writes in the active voice	• I got it. • I have some questions. • I am unsure.	

Figure 5.5: Take-a-stand criteria and student-confidence-rating reflection.

Demonstrating Quality and Not-So-Quality Work

As students begin to understand the language of the learning, we ask them to examine strong and weak examples of work (Chappuis, 2009). During a middle school math collaborative meeting, one teacher described how she had asked students to work in groups to assess anonymous student problem solving. After scoring each sample against a rubric, students needed to come to consensus on their scoring using evidence from the problem to defend their position. They were then given an "expert" opinion, an analysis of that student work provided by the U.S. Department of State, which they compared to their own interpretations. As a result, students began to have a clearer idea of what quality work looks like through engaging in an analysis of other student's work.

In *Motivating Students: 25 Strategies to Light the Fire of Engagement*, Carolyn Chapman and I (2011) articulate a strategy of co-constructing rubrics with students. We provide a number of examples of work, and students put the samples in order from best to worst. From there, learners describe what makes the work quality. This becomes the foundation of the rubric. While this activity takes time, it also acts as an instructional lesson and creates a picture of quality that is deeper than one that comes from handing students a preconstructed rubric.

Amanda Smith, a fourth-grade teacher in Newfoundland, describes an activity that helped students explore strong and weak examples.

> The activity that presented the most discussion was what I called the "Mixed-Up Sticky Notes." I gave the students four mini test papers that they had completed and a blank piece of paper with four sticky notes labeled A, B, C, and D. Each sticky note had the correct and incorrect responses of each of the mini tests. The challenge for each group was to figure out what sticky note belonged with what paper. They had a lot of fun and engaged in a lot of discussion. Of course, they had to first figure out the correct answers, then apply the knowledge accordingly. It was great fun and great learning! (A. Smith, personal communication, May 10, 2010)

These examples create a picture of how to build students' understanding of the learning goals—both in language and in work.

Providing Descriptive Feedback

My daughter, Maya, is a creative child who has little patience for details. It's the creative endeavor that gets her excited and committed to learning. In her early elementary years, she received the same type of feedback on most of her work: "Creative and juicy details. Watch your capital letters, periods, and sentences." Her fourth-grade teacher changed this pattern with one simple but powerful action. It was the first reading assessment, and it provided open-ended questions. Maya got her paper back with the same feedback— "strong details" and then the now-familiar "watch your sentence structure." However, this time, the teacher required students to go back and revise their work. By that simple instructional strategy, revision, Maya's writing improved dramatically in two weeks. Was she happy about having to revise? Not so much. But that kind of practice leads to improvement and makes it stick. John Hattie and Helen Timperley (2007) find that this type of revision leads to higher achievement as opposed to offering feedback and then expecting students to apply those comments to the next task.

There are various purposes for feedback. In some cases, feedback is used to rationalize a score or proficiency level. But feedback may also be used to inspire learning. Inspiring feedback provides direction to the student regarding how to improve. I used to get frustrated when students would make the same mistake over and over again. Reflecting back, I was expecting students to transfer those insightful comments I made on their work or in our conversation to the next time they encountered that type of work.

For feedback to be successful, consider the following.

- **Be descriptive:** Avoid quantities or general comments like "try again" or "add more." Use descriptive language that tells students about the qualities of their work.

- **Be purposeful:** When providing feedback to improve achievement, your comments should promote learning, not simply justify a score.

- **Begin with a strength:** Then offer a next step.

- **Build in time and learning:** Students need these to take action on your comments.

- **Less is more:** Offer students fewer assignments and assessments but more opportunities to use your comments to revise and develop their work.

- **Focus on one or two areas, learning goals, or criteria:** Too many comments overwhelm students, and they don't know where to start.

- **Prompt students to action:** Don't fix their mistakes for them. Students are often confused when the teacher writes over their work, fixing it for them, and don't see where the misunderstanding occurred.

Hattie and Timperley (2007) review countless feedback studies and offer insight into the types of feedback that support learning. They conclude that quality descriptive feedback should lead to students gaining deeper understanding of what constitutes quality work. Although initially they will be more dependent on feedback to revise and learn from their mistakes, eventually they will be able to recognize their strengths and take the next steps toward improvement more independently, as they build toward student investment. Any descriptive comment offered by teachers should require action or reflection by the students, leading to students being able to more independently self-assess.

One traditional classroom practice is to hand the work back to the students with comments and a grade and expect them to learn from the feedback and transfer that learning to the next assignment. This transfer of learning doesn't happen often unless students are *required* to act on the comments and improve their work (Hattie, 2009; Hattie & Timperley, 2007; Wiliam, 2007). In a context where grading is communicating about learning, students use the comments to revise their writing and make it stronger. This is teaching students responsibility in meaningful ways that makes learning last beyond the paper and supports students' achievement not only on a standardized test, but in their lives. It teaches them how to persevere until they see quality. Students who don't turn something in may be required to complete the work as the class begins. If there is additional time built in to the day, the student works on the assignment then, or it becomes homework again. But it is vitally important to understand the root cause of the work not being completed. If a student didn't do the assignment because he or she was overwhelmed and didn't know where to start, asking that student to do it again won't produce a different result. Instead, that student may need to have the assignment broken into segmented steps that he or she can do independently. For students to move forward, a teacher must not only require that the work be done but also address the reasons it was not.

Many teachers will lament the lack of time for this kind of response—so it is important to note again that the work being assigned is vitally important and worth spending this much time on; in fact, I would argue that we should assign *only* things that are vitally important and that must be revised, fixed, and examined. Less is more—this means having our students do more with fewer assignments. In this way, we are drastically reducing paperwork for teachers and increasing the work that students must do to improve, practice, and achieve success.

Feedback can come in a variety of forms, Hattie and Timperley (2007) review the effect of the following four types of feedback: personal feedback, task or product feedback, process feedback, and feedback to self.

Personal Feedback

Personal feedback is the type of feedback least likely to connect learning to student performance. This kind of feedback, in which the learners make their own assumptions about why the teacher said "good" or "try harder," may be interpreted by students as a judgment on their self-worth. This kind of feedback is easy to provide but has little or negative effects on student achievement. Examples include:

- "Fantastic presentation!"
- "Good job!"
- Simply a smiley face (☺)

Task or Product Feedback

Task or product feedback usually addresses the correctness or incorrectness of a response and tells students how to make a specific task better or fix a mistake. This type of feedback is more effective when addressing misconceptions and asking students to understand their misconceptions and fix their mistakes with newfound insight. It can be offered to individuals or groups in written or verbal form and is most effective when offered with simplicity and specificity. Task or product feedback has a moderate effect on student learning. Examples include:

- "Add examples and explanations to support your description of the character as smart."
- "Add more information about what led to Emmett Till's tragedy."
- "Explain how the quotation from Oates's poem 'Dreaming America' supports your claim that the American dream is an ideal and not a reality."

Process Feedback

Process feedback consists of comments that address the process students use to understand or produce their work (such as a writing process, problem-solving strategy, or reading strategy). The goal here is to guide the learner to automaticity, the stage at which he or she begins to internalize the process and move toward self-regulation and self-assessment. This means students can independently recognize quality and lack of quality in their work. Comments associated with this type of feedback focus on asking students to analyze their errors, make corrections, and revisit a specific aspect of the process in order to revise their work. When process feedback is connected to student goal setting, it's quite effective and has the potential to significantly affect student learning. Examples include:

- "Review the definition of an inference and different ways we find them. Choose one method, and use it to find the inference in the first section of the reading."
- "Review the tips for creating effective PowerPoint slides. Revise your slides to reflect those tips."
- "Consider the criteria for critiquing a mathematicians' problem solving, provide one more critique of the problem solving illustrated in problem 5."

Feedback to Self

Feedback to self, also called self-assessment and self-regulation, is focused on the student using what he or she already knows to make adjustments. Learners assess their work in relation to the bigger goal (rubric) or in comparison to strong work (writing samples, effective solutions) and make plans to revise or fix it based on their own findings. This type of feedback may involve learners who recognize that they need help but are asking for hints more than answers. Self-assessment and self-regulation are the epitome of student investment and have a significant effect on student learning. Examples include:

- "Review your unit 1 math test, and identify your strengths (what you know and feel confident about) and analyze your errors to identify the math concepts you need to work on."
- "Use the writing rubric to self-assess your work (both strengths and focus areas). Provide examples to support your rating."

The Issue of Time

Time is often described as one of the biggest obstacles to providing effective, descriptive feedback that students learn from. Wiliam (2008) describes cycles of responding to assessment information. Table 5.3 is designed to generate conversation around the types of assessments and instruction that can promote learning and the time frame it takes to respond to the information. As teachers consider what kinds of practices fall into the various time frames; it is helpful to think about what the teacher is doing and how he or she is using the information, as well as how the students are investing in it. This is a tool for teachers to intentionally plan moments when they are using formative assessment or responding to student learning needs, as well as when the student is taking action—the most critical aspect of students learning more.

Table 5.3: Teacher and Student Practices Over Short, Medium, and Long Time Frames

Time Frame	Teacher Practices	Student-Investment Practices
Long cycle • **Span:** Across units, terms • **Length:** Four weeks to one year • **Impact:** Student monitoring; curriculum alignment	Teachers change curriculum, units, or instructional activities to better support student learning.	Student reflection on the overall effectiveness of instruction and assessment informs changes for the next year.
Medium cycle • **Span:** Within and between teaching units • **Length:** One to four weeks • **Impact:** Improved, student investment, assessment; teacher cognition about learning	Teachers use intentionally focused, more formal assessment that measures the hard-to-teach, hard-to-learn, essential-to-know learning goals. Teachers analyze most common mistakes on a quiz, for example, and plan instruction; comments on papers or student work direct instruction.	Students engage in fixing mistakes, revising their work or engaging in activities based on how they responded to a more formal formative assessment such as a quiz or a rough draft. Students engage in self-assessment and tracking progress on essential standards.
Short cycle • **Span:** Within and between lessons • **Length:** Day by day—twenty-four to forty-eight hours; minute by minute—five seconds to two hours • **Impact:** Classroom practice; student engagement	Teachers ask questions and lead activities based on observations of students understanding and misconceptions. Teachers may gather exit slips or ask students to offer a thumbs up or thumbs down to indicate understanding. Based on responses, teachers do something immediately or the next day.	Students are talking, writing, and working based on their comments and work in the midst of instruction.

Consider the following four tips in addressing time in the context of descriptive feedback and promoting student investment. These practices are designed so students start to do more self-reflection.

Phrase Rubrics in Positive Language. When rubrics are written in deficit language, it is much more difficult for students to use them to make revisions and move forward. But if they contain positive language, a student who gets a rubric score of 2 knows that is a strength and looks to find out the next level of strength. See chapter 4 (page 45) for more on quality rubrics.

Write Short Descriptive Comments for Students to Self-Assess. Students review their own work and select the comment that best matches what they need to work on. In essence, students are giving themselves feedback on their work. Sample comments might come from previous student work, used anonymously; from student work sites such as Looking at Student Work (www.lasw.org); from teacher-written samples; or from video segments from TeacherTube or YouTube. In addition, the on-standard (often level 3) descriptions provide great statements when written in the positive form to use for creating student investment, as shown in figures 5.6 and 5.7 for elementary reading comprehension strategies and high school math, respectively.

Criteria	Directions: Star your strength. Circle your next step.	How and when will you take this next step? What help or support do you need to act on your next step?
Elementary Reading Comprehension Strategies		
Make Connections (prior knowledge)	• Relates background knowledge and experience to text (This reminds me . . . This happened in another story I read . . . I remember a movie . . .) • Uses schema to expand interpretation of text—this means students might draw a picture to connect ideas, characters, or text structure, or use words to explain those connections	
Question	• Asks questions to clarify meaning • Asks questions that get one thinking about the text (not just what the text says, but questions that suggest deeper meaning or connections or ideas) • Asks questions that challenge the text or critique the text • Uses evidence from the text to pose these questions	
Infer	• Makes predictions about the text or characters • Draws conclusions about the text—theme, characters, or impact (nonfiction) • Explains the source of the conclusion or prediction	
Synthesize	• Reflects on the meaning of the text • Uses own schema to enhance meaning • Identifies themes of text along with evidence or schema that reflects those themes	

Figure 5.6: Elementary reading feedback for self-assessment.

Criteria	Directions: Star your strength. Circle your next step.	How and when will you take this next step? What help or support do you need to act on your next step?
High School Math		
Demonstrates Mathematical Knowledge	• Executes mathematical algorithms completely and accurately • Uses accurate notation and mathematical terminology • Confidently shows understanding of the mathematical concepts required	
Provides Solutions	• Identifies all elements of the problem • Shows relationships among elements • Clearly shows systematic problem-solving strategy	
Explains Mathematics	• Uses mathematical terminology to justify solution and strategy or counterstrategy and solution • Uses appropriate diagram and describes elements • Provides examples or counterexamples to explain solution	

Figure 5.7: High school math feedback for self-assessment.

Embed Descriptive Feedback in Instruction. The powerful part of feedback is the action taken. Quality comments should lead to thinking and cause action (Wiliam, 2011). As a result, consider building that action into your lessons and instruction. The following protocol is an example of this practice in a music classroom.

1. Show a video clip of a rehearsal or a concert. Model how to offer descriptive feedback to the group. The descriptive feedback could be focused on any criterion or aspect of the performance that needs work—for example, dynamics or intonation. The key is engaging students in a discussion of what varying levels of tone sounds like and acquainting them with key actions that can improve tone.

2. Show a video clip of an individual student playing, singing, or performing. Ask students to write down their feedback. They then discuss what was strong about the performance and what actions the student might take to improve. Engage students in sharing their ideas and help them improve their understanding of what the descriptive feedback focused on.

3. Show three or four clips, and ask students individually and in groups to provide descriptive feedback on the clip as a way to give students language around self-assessing their own performance.

4. Move to having students self-assess their own performance using the same criteria. It is helpful to record and post descriptive feedback so students can use it to self-assess their own work.

Write Descriptive Feedback in Collaboration With Colleagues or Students. This is a five-step process for teachers in collaborative teams to engage in to use the ideas of descriptive feedback to plan instructional responses. The process could also be used with students as an instructional activity to learn the criteria and revise their work.

1. Identify six to eight random student work samples (remove names and use letters or numbers).

2. Each person on the team writes *strengths* (description of what learning is demonstrated) and *action steps* (a comment to improve the work) for each piece of work. Sticky notes work well for each person to identify the strength and next step without seeing each other's comments.

3. Each person shares his or her strengths and action steps, and the group comes to consensus on the strengths and action steps for each student.

4. Referring back to the four types of feedback (pages 91), each person identifies the type of feedback they wrote for each student and makes adjustments to craft statements that will help students grow rather than shut them down.

5. The team decides how they will offer the statements to students and what they will do with the action steps. Will those students with the same action steps meet together to revise their work? Will there be a minilesson from the teacher, after which the students work independently to revise and improve? The team decides based on its structure and student needs.

Figure 5.8 shows a template that can be used for teachers to record the strengths and next steps. The team generates a few comments (strengths and next steps) based on the six to eight samples they reviewed. They write the comments on the template, and then copy it multiple times. Teachers review the rest of their student work and then sort the work in piles based on the strength and next step each student needs to achieve. Teachers can then easily jot the student's name down on the appropriate comment, instead of writing new comments on every paper. Students receive those slips, plan their action steps, and make their revisions. This process helps focus the teachers' comments and also requires students to work hard versus the teachers doing all of those revisions and working harder than the student. This approach also avoids the tendency for those insights written by teachers to fall in the trash and not be used by students to improve. While this protocol is designed for a team to focus their comments and not provide too much information, individual teachers can also engage in it to focus their individual descriptive feedback practice.

```
Name: _____

Strength:

Next Step:

Action Taken:
```

Figure 5.8: Form for descriptive feedback and student self-assessment.

Visit **go.solution-tree.com/assessment** for a reproducible form of this figure.

Purposeful Feedback to Teachers

What we intend students to hear and experience is very different than how they are actually perceiving it. That is why we need to hear from them. Hattie (2009), in *Visible Learning: A Synthesis of Over 800 Meta-Analyses Relating to Achievement*, suggests that some of the most valuable feedback is from students to teachers. Carol Rodgers (2006) writes of "the power of students' description of their own learning as revealed to teachers in dialogue, a process I call descriptive feedback, in meeting learners' needs and in building trust and community" (p. 210).

When students trust the teacher and the culture of the classroom, they are more likely to take risks and engage even when they might not be sure of the purpose. They will engage because they trust that the teacher has their best interests in mind, knowing that relevance and meaning will come. Mei Schulte (2009), as a senior in high school, describes the power of listening in her essay on learning.

> She [the teacher] has such a strong ability to put me at ease, along with several of the other people I know who have had her. When anyone says anything and she doesn't understand, she says, "Go on, what do you mean by this?" She really wants to know us as more than just students and that is rare to see in high school. Whenever she used to bring up new policies that maybe didn't seem fair to us she would say, "You can argue it out with me after class, I am open to hearing what you think." . . . The fact that she has an open ear really makes her that much more amiable. (p. 3)

The simple act of asking and listening builds trust—something essential if students are to invest. Following are several ways to give and receive feedback.

Exit Slips. Feedback from students to teachers can also come in the form of exit slips, on which students make comments or rate a class activity. For example, you could create a simple exit slip for students with the student's name and the name of the activity, asking the following.

- What was the best part of the activity, and why?
- What was the most challenging aspect of the activity, and why?
- What did you learn?
- What would you do differently if you could do it over again?
- What recommendations do you have for changing the way the activity is done next time?

Student Confidence Checks. Marking stars and check marks is a common practice on work produced by students. While I must admit, I look for the stars and words like "Great!" to appear on the work of my children as an affirmation that they are doing what they need to do; scoring schemes that describe more about what that star means—beyond that they got the right answer and it was neat—create a culture focused on learning. Points and grades are game changers. What once was doing work to learn becomes about gathering points, or getting stars. What if, on these daily assignments, there were a description of learning goals and a scale describing the extent to which the work reflected this goal. For example, a first-grade assessment asked students to find all the temperature gauges in the house, draw them, and then do a few problems to assess greater than and less than. What if there were an arrow on the top of the paper where the student marked the extent of his or her confidence about that learning goal and the teacher commented on or affirmed that confidence rating? It might look something like figure 5.9.

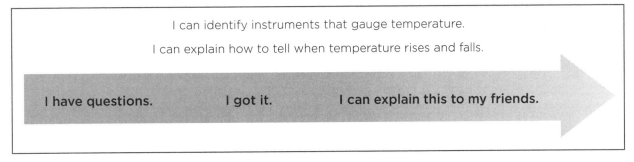

Figure 5.9: Student confidence check.

Surveys. Student feedback to teachers can also happen through more formal means, such as a survey. Sometimes I use a survey form that students can fill out anonymously. Teachers then review it and reflect on what is strong about the classroom practice and what changes might make a difference for students and their learning. The statements in the survey are designed to inform teachers' practice, not to evaluate their effectiveness. Visit **go.solution-tree.com/assessment** to download a copy of this tool.

Focus Groups. Feedback can also come in the form of a focus group. I have younger students place stickers on a Likert scale (figure 5.10) in response to various statements and then facilitate dialogue with students to discuss their responses. One statement that I frequently pose is, "Comments on my paper help me learn."

Figure 5.10: Student comments using stickers on a Likert scale.

A few key patterns have emerged over the years that tell teachers which feedback practices are most effective according to students. Those students who placed stickers on the "strongly disagree" side said that teachers wrote over their work or solved problems for them. They often couldn't figure out how the teacher had gone from their work to the "right" answer. Other students stated that there were so many comments they did not know where to start. On the "strongly agree" side, students described moments when teachers asked them questions and gave them time to respond and revise. Although they didn't always like having to do more, they affirmed that those types of comments helped them learn. It is always amazing to see the incredibly insightful comments that students pose and how much they mirror the research I often cite.

Descriptive feedback does more than promote and support learning—it builds relationships with students and creates a positive culture in a classroom. Citing a paper Matt Deevers (2006) presents to the American Educational Research Association, Dylan Wiliam (2011) notes that "a study of 1,571 students in 84 mathematics classrooms from fifth to twelfth grades found that students provided with positive constructive feedback by their teachers were more likely to focus on learning rather than performance" (p. 151). When students know they had a hand in structuring that feedback, they take it even more seriously and that promotes student investment.

Self-Reflecting, Setting Goals, and Taking Action

Goal setting has great potential to inspire and promote learning in students (Hattie, 2009; Hattie & Timperley, 2007; Marzano, 2006, 2007). A key element of effective goal-setting practices is being specific—both in terms of evaluating strengths and in setting objectives. In the absence of a clear idea of the criteria for quality work or learning goals, students set superficial goals.

Charting progress is one common example of self-reflecting and setting goals to foster student investment. In some cases, students plot their progress over time on certain skills. This provides a visual that can be a powerful motivator (Hattie, 2009; Marzano, 2010). In the next section, students work on one high-powered (essential for future success) skill multiple times over the year or unit, depending on the time frame. In the three examples that follow, students are using rubrics to track their scores, setting goals, and taking action to learn more in between assessments.

Example 1: Charting Reading Progress

When teachers identify essential standards or learning goals that are addressed across units and over time, it is an opportunity to create a rubric and then ask students to track their achievement on multiple tasks or assessments. Figure 5.11 shows a graph that could be used for students to track their progress on a reading standard over time. This rubric is used to assess various tasks on different texts that students are reading. Their response is scored on the rubric and charted each time on the graph.

Example 2: Charting Science and Math Data Analysis

Like the reading chart in figure 5.11, figure 5.12 (page 100) illustrates a rubric and a tracking template for data analysis. The key to tracking is to target a standard or skill that occurs over time. As students engage in assessments and practice that targeted skill, such as data analysis, it becomes a visual representation students can use to reflect on how they are progressing. Students often find the visual an effective way to begin to make connections to their work and their learning. This tracking provides information for setting goals and making plans to improve between assessments.

I can summarize. This means I can identify the main idea and the most important details that support the main idea.	
4	With deep understanding of the text, makes connections to other texts, experiences, or concepts
3	Accurately identifies the implied main idea; specific details are used to explain and support the main idea
2	Accurately identifies the implied main idea; specific details are taken directly from the text, but it's not clear how the specific details support the main idea
1	Describes ideas from the text without identifying the main idea

"I Can" Statements	Date	Date	Date	Date	Date	Date	Date	Date	Date	Date
I can summarize. This means I can identify the main idea and the most important details that support the main idea.										

Figure 5.11: Four-point rubric for tracking reading comprehension over time with student self-assessment.

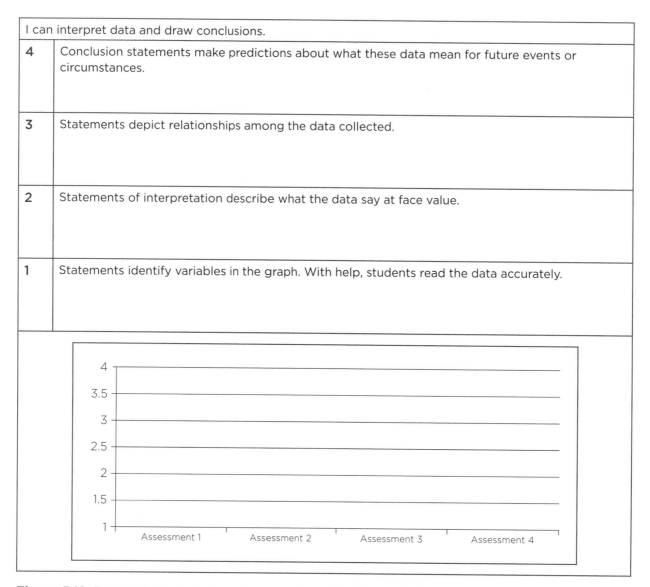

	I can interpret data and draw conclusions.
4	Conclusion statements make predictions about what these data mean for future events or circumstances.
3	Statements depict relationships among the data collected.
2	Statements of interpretation describe what the data say at face value.
1	Statements identify variables in the graph. With help, students read the data accurately.

Figure 5.12: Four-point rubric for science and math data analysis with student self-assessment.

Example 3: Reading Fluency Template

In the next three-step example (figure 5.13), students are first asked to consider key elements of what it means to read fluently. This question ensures that students go beyond simply tracking the number of words they can read to consider what it means to be a reader. The example also provides prompting for students to reflect and then set goals for improvement throughout the year.

Name: <u>Giorgio</u>

Step 1: Define reading fluency.

I am working on my reading fluency. Reading fluency is . . .

Note: Teachers can lead students in a brief conversation about reading fluency and students can write, draw, or copy what it is. Things like:

- *The number of words I can read per minute—as I improve in reading, I can read faster. Reading faster helps us understand some kinds of text.*

- *The expression or emotion I use in reading—when I read faster and smoother, I can start to stress different parts of a sentence and use emotion (quieter, louder, joy, sadness, pausing) to help show what the reading means.*

- *There are times when I want to read slower and reread something to better understand the meaning of the text.*

The reading fluency benchmark assessment gives me information about my progress on fluency—what I am good at and what next step will help me improve. My score tells me how many words I read per minute. There are goals for the overall grade I am in that help me decide what I can do to grow and keep getting better. I get to set goals for my individual progress, too.

How do we get better at reading fluency? Teachers and students brainstorm ideas so that as students look at their score, they have ideas about what it means and how they can get better.

Step 2: Shade in the graph to show how many words you read per minute each time.

Timing	Fall	Winter	Spring
100			
90			
80			
70			
60			
50			
40			
30			
20			
10			
0			
Score	20	62	80

Figure 5.13: Reading comprehension student tracking and goal setting.

Continued on next page →

Step 3: Set goals and make plans to grow.

	Fall Reflection	Winter Reflection	Spring Reflection
Strengths (Can take from step 1—what reading fluency is)	I read 20 words per minute.	I read 62 words per minute, and this is a strength. Reading words is pretty simple. I'm getting better at reading with emotion.	I read 80 words per minute, and I'm getting much better at reading with emotion to show meaning. I understand some of what I read.
Challenges (Can take from step 1—what reading fluency is)	I need to read with more emotion and meaning.	I need to work on reading and then being able to remember or talk about what the reading means.	I need to work on being able to summarize what I'm reading both in writing and by just talking.
Next Steps to Improve (Can take from step 1—how to get better and grow)	I'm going to practice re-reading in my reading group. I'm going to audio tape myself and then try again. We will check in with our reading groups after two weeks to see if we have improved.	I'm going to write questions and sentences about what I read in my reading group. We will check in with our reading groups after two weeks to see if we have improved.	We are working on this in our reading groups. I'm going to practice during reading groups.

Visit **go.solution-tree.com/assessment** for a blank reproducible version of this figure.

Put Phase Five Into Play

Phase five is where the whole assessment comes together. The items, tasks, and rubrics are created and intentionally aligned to the cognitive level in the standards, the documents and materials are organized, and there is a plan of how to use the information to foster student investment. The following is the complete summative assessment for the American dream unit that includes an overall scoring sheet by learning goal, the actual items and tasks, and a student self-reflection. This assessment has three parts and will be administered on three separate days. The American dream assessment is found in figure 5.14.

The Ninth-Grade American Dream Assessment: How Has the American Dream Changed Over Time?

Name: _____ Date: _____

Part 1: Constructed Response

Learning Goal: I can compare and contrast key messages in multiple texts on the same topic.

We have been exploring the following question: "How has the American dream changed over time and how does that influence my world?

We have read "I Hear America Singing," by Walt Whitman, and "Winter Dreams," by F. Scott Fitzgerald. We have also read a survey on the American dream (Center for the Study of the American Dream, 2014).

For this task, read "Dreaming America," by Joyce Carol Oates, and view the NBC news clip describing and questioning the state of the American dream (Linn, 2013).

Given the information in the article and the video, describe the key messages and how they develop. Explain your thinking using evidence from the text and video. In addition, compare and contrast the two pieces, again using evidence to support your thinking.

Criteria	Total Points Achieved
I can determine the central idea or theme in a text.	_____/10 (5 points per text)
I can analyze the details that lead to the theme over the course of a text. This means I use text evidence to support my ideas and explain them well.	_____/10 (5 points per text)
I can produce an objective summary of a text.	_____/10 (5 points per text)
I can compare and contrast key messages in multiple texts on the same topic.	_____/20 (10 points per text)
I can effectively use written language to communicate my ideas.	_____/10 (5 points per text)
Overall Total Points Achieved	_____/60 points

Part 2: Socratic Dialogue

The Socratic dialogue will be assessed using the following rubric. Points will be assigned for each criterion. During the formative assessment stages, there are no points assigned and students use the rubric to plan how to improve.

Figure 5.14: Complete summative assessment for the American dream unit.

Continued on next page →

Criteria	1—Beginning	2—Emerging	3—Proficient	4—Distinguished
Questioning (20 points)	• I can ask questions to clarify what the text means.	• I can pose questions that reference the text.	• I can pose questions that emerge directly from text evidence. • I can pose questions to clarify a peer's contribution.	• I can use multiple contributions to pose deeper-level questions.
Expressing Ideas (20 points)	• I can summarize ideas from the text.	• I can express my ideas clearly with loose connections to the text.	• I can express my ideas clearly and persuasively using text evidence. • I can summarize points of agreement and disagreement.	• I can make new connections from evidence and reasoning in the dialogue.
Generating Ideas (20 points)	• I can reiterate what someone else said.	• I can respond to questions in a dialogue.	• I can use evidence from the text to generate dialogue. • I can build on others' ideas.	• I can pose questions and comments that help the dialogue go deeper.

Students will submit their notes and a self-reflection of how they feel they engaged in the Socratic dialogue using the sample rubric as a guide for this reflection.

Following the Socratic dialogue, students will then submit answers to the following using Google Docs.

- Which criteria do you feel was your strength? Explain why, and use specific examples from the dialogue.

- Which criteria do you feel you need to work on? What could you do differently next time to improve those areas?

- What was the most memorable part of the dialogue? Describe the moment and why you think it was memorable.

- Describe a comment or part of the dialogue that helped you gain a new perspective on the American dream and any of the pieces we read or viewed.

- Describe a comment or question in the dialogue that pushed your thinking or challenged you.

Part 3: Podcast

The podcast will be assessed using the following criteria. Students will indicate their assessment of each criterion with a simple *yes*, *no*, or *sometimes*. Students will explain their response using specific examples from their podcast.

Student Response	Criteria	Teacher Score (each element receives 5 points)
	Provides a clear and focused argument	
	Develops argument effectively (effective textual evidence that is explained well)	
	Contains multiple sources	
	Provides accurate interpretations of texts	
	Uses language and vocabulary effectively	
	Voice and expression is effective in delivering the message	

Visit **go.solution-tree.com/assessment** for a reproducible form of this figure.

Pause and Ponder

The following questions are designed to help individual teachers or teams focus on the essential ideas presented in this chapter.

- Consider the key elements and practices of student investment (page 86–87). Any of those practices in isolation can help students learn. However, if they are going to create a culture of learning that promotes students being invested in their work and taking more ownership to get better, they must be *used* purposefully. In what ways do those practices build that kind of investment?

- Consider the type of feedback students currently receive most often. How much of it is strength based? How much is pointing to next steps? How often are students invited versus required to act on that feedback? Based on your dialogue, what are your strengths and next steps in using feedback to promote learning?

- What kind of feedback might be most useful to gather from students?

- What kind of high-powered skills might be useful and meaningful for students to track? Consider learning goals that emerge in multiple places throughout units or the year.

- What are the key aspects of phase five in relationship to grading and scoring? Why might offering students a scoring scheme that reflects learning support an assessment-rich culture?

- Another great task for departments or grade levels is reviewing their homework and grading policies. In this process, each individual teacher would bring his or her policy to the table and the team would talk about the intention behind the policies and what they hope to accomplish with the policies. When considering Reeves's call for grading practices that are accurate, fair, specific, and timely, a school grade level or department might review how its policies meet and don't meet the criteria. This includes describing different ways in which these policies are applied. Using this information to further define grading policies and recording and reporting policies will move your work forward.

Collaborating to Create Assessments

When spider webs unite, they can tie up a lion.

—African Proverb

The Design in Five process, outlined in the first five chapters of this book, leads to meaningful and engaging assessment practices. While the process can be used by individual teachers, there is power in collaborating with colleagues to create engaging assessments and use information to help students learn more and invest in their learning. Through dialogue during the phases, a deeper understanding of what we want students to learn emerges and a culture of learning in classrooms and schools is created. Collaborating with colleagues to tap into the expertise of the group can be a powerful means for finding innovative solutions that help all students learn at high levels. This chapter defines common assessment practice and structures of assessment in collaboration and offers tools that describe common assessment work and implementation plans to ensure engaging assessments and high levels of learning.

Define Common Assessment Practice

Cassandra Erkens (2013), a leading assessment expert, defines a common assessment in the following way.

> A collaborative common assessment is any assessment, both formative and summative in design, that is team created or team endorsed by teachers who share standard expectations; it must be designed in advance of instruction and administered in close proximity by all instructors who share a role in administering that assessment; those who designed or endorsed the assessment must then collaboratively examine the results for consistent scoring and shared, instructionally sensitive responses that address the following:
>
> - Error analysis and appropriate instructional planning for individual students
> - Curriculum, instruction, and/or assessment modifications. (p. 19)

Teams of teachers work together to understand and interpret the standards. Part of this is considering the student work that will reflect the standard. Common assessments are not designed to take away creativity or freedom in a teacher's practice. The team must develop a shared understanding of learning that is expected in their courses or grade level. Some evidence needs to be common in order to ensure a coherent, aligned, intentional school experience for our students. However, there is much flexibility and creativity in the way teachers and students work and interact together to achieve those standards. Common assessment work in this collaborative way is about tapping into the expertise of the individuals on the team on skills that are difficult but essential for students to understand to be successful in future coursework and in the world in which they live. Through collaboration, teams design engaging assessments to reflect standards and examine results and student work to attend to students' learning needs. This kind of professional dialogue creates a culture of learning for both teachers and students.

Build Structures to Assess Collaboratively

There are a number of structures for teachers to consider when collaborating on assessment. Grade-level teams or departments should weigh their options and then commit to work regularly in one of the following models.

- The entire grade-level team or department focuses on a skill that crosses content areas or appears vertically throughout the course sequence, such as writing, inquiring, problem solving, collaborating, or reading. In this model, the team develops some general criteria with the possibility of disciplines adding content-specific aspects of the skill. In reviewing the assessment data, individual teachers would, in turn, bring in examples of their student work for the team to review. Each time the focus would be on the skill, but within a different content area. For example, a department that consists of classes such as accounting, word processing, and family and consumer science reviews its standards and learning goals and may find a key concept such as ethics or communication that crosses all courses.

- Teams of teachers who teach the same course or grade level meet and articulate the learning goals, develop assessments, and analyze and plan instructional responses based on common formative assessment data. In this model, it is essential that teams not only plan when they will administer the common formative assessment, but also when they will respond.

- Teachers find teams or other teachers to collaborate with online. Casey Rutherford is a physics teacher in Shakopee, Minnesota (http://learningandphysics.wordpress.com/about). He put out a call to physics teachers around the country and created his own online professional learning community. (See www.allthingsplc.info for more connections and deeper ideas on creating effective professional learning communities.)

Whatever model you use, the most powerful aspect of collaboration is to analyze the data or student work and go back to the classroom and differentiate instruction and engage students in learning based on those findings.

Plan a Sequence of Collaborative Team Meetings

To move the work of common formative assessments forward, teams—after determining their structure— identify learning goals and develop a common formative assessment that they will analyze at a collaborative meeting and use to plan an instructional response (intervention). This means that the teams plan in advance when to administer a short common formative assessment, when they will analyze the results together, and when they will go back and respond in order to help the students learn more on the targeted learning goal. In the absence of this kind of planning, teams may feel overwhelmed by the process. The timing and sequence of meetings might look something like this:

1. At the first meeting, determine the next three meeting times (where assessment is the focus), identify the learning goals that will be addressed in the next few weeks, choose a learning goal or two, and create a short assessment that the team agrees to administer before the next meeting. The learning goals chosen should be essential to know, hard to teach, and hard to learn.

2. At the second meeting, each member of the team brings student work from the common assessment (agreed on in the first meeting), and the team analyzes the data and plans an instructional response that it will implement prior to the next meeting. This meeting may benefit from having an outside facilitator to guide and focus the conversation in order to produce a plan until the team feels confident about making the plan.

3. At meeting three, the team debriefs the impact of the instructional response (perhaps a short follow-up formative assessment is created and administered to see if any change occurred in student learning). The cycle repeats as often as doable.

This cycle can work no matter how often the teams meet. If it is every two weeks, then the teams just pay attention to learning goals that will be most relevant over the course of that instruction. If the teams meet once a month, the targeted skill to be formatively assessed must be high powered and relevant for students to address across time and units, such as drawing conclusions from data or citing textual evidence to support a claim. Students would benefit from making revisions to their work in both of these areas a week or two after they had written the first draft. When there is more time between meetings, the targeted learning goal must be high priority and essential to student success in their future units, grade levels, and course work.

Create a Common Assessment Calendar

A common assessment calendar can help a team organize how to best use common formative assessments to inform learning. So often, assessment information, when analyzed in collaboration, is no longer relevant because the time to respond to the information has passed.

The sample common assessment weekly calendar shown in figure 6.1 (page 110) can be used if you meet weekly (or monthly, by changing the row headers to month 1, month 2, and so on). However often you meet, the most important aspect of the planning is analyzing the student work and data and planning an instructional response.

If common assessments that are intended to be formative turn out to be summative, meaning the data are analyzed but no response is employed, then the work of common assessments becomes more about documentation than about providing information to inform learning and practice. When this happens, teachers are often collecting a lot of data and doing a lot of assessment without building in time for the response. This leads to teachers often feeling overwhelmed and drowning in data. For example, if the common assessment is given on Monday and the team meets a week later but the information becomes out of date and there is no plan to build instruction into lesson planning based on the formative data, the process becomes more challenging, less supportive to teachers, and less effective in bringing about an increase in student learning. In these situations, teachers often report feeling that common formative assessments add layers of work to an already full plate. Timing is essential, and so effective implementation involves planning when the assessment will be administered, when the team will meet to analyze and design the instructional response, and when the response will occur. This type of process helps the team see the work of common assessments as supportive to its lesson planning and not something added to what it already does.

Date	Task	Who	Expected Outcome
Week 1	• Reflect on effectiveness of last week's response. • Determine focus learning goals (derived from essential standards). • Plan, design, and choose a short common formative assessment to be administered next week.	Whole Team Sydney will bring an assessment she used last year for us to review and revise.	Team decides on the standard, learning goals, or both for the common formative assessment (phases one and two of Design in Five)
Week 2	• Continue planning and designing common formative assessment to be administered this week. • Administer the assessment.	Whole Team	Team leaves with a crafted assessment (phases three and four of Design in Five) and an agreement to administer the common formative assessment before the next meeting
Week 3	• Bring student work from the assessment to the team meeting to calibrate scoring, or bring assessment scores and combine into a document to be analyzed. • Score, analyze, and plan instructional response to data.	Whole Team	Team leaves with an instructional response to be carried out the next day during math literacy centers (phase five of Design in Five)
Week 4	• Continue planning response (if needed). • Assess the effectiveness of the response. • Begin the cycle again with week 1.	Whole Team	Team leaves with a better understanding of the effectiveness of the instructional response and begins to decide on the next learning goal to formatively assess together

Figure 6.1: Sample common assessment weekly calendar.

Visit **go.solution-tree.com/assessment** or page 143 for a blank reproducible form of this figure.

The power of collaborative teams coming together resides not only in supporting student learning, but also in improving a teacher's practice and clarity around learning—in terms of both the work required and the way we score and communicate. One middle school math professional learning community had the following experience:

> I just came from a very exciting 7th grade math PLC (professional learning community) meeting. I brought data to the table about a recent formative and summative test they had given to the students. Everyone was very open about the data. (YAY!!!!) However, there was quite a discrepancy between one teacher's formative test data and the other teachers. (His was a lot lower.) I had sent everyone the data the day before so everyone could digest the data prior to the meeting. So the first thing this teacher said was, "Let's talk about the white elephant in the room." So we talked about it. The teacher brought his tests and we figured out that he graded differently than the others. So I opened the door to using the grading (calibration) protocol you gave us next PLC to see how everyone will grade the next formative. We are doing it. I am so excited! (personal communication, September 16, 2010)

For collaborative groups to work well, there must be a safe place to share what is working and what is not.

Implement Collaborative Assessment Work

Describing what a collaborative team will be doing as team members meet together is essential in order to move beyond just relying on teachers' past experience in implementing these practices. This section contains a list of eight steps needed to understand common assessment work. In some cases, collaborative teams self-assess their understanding and implementation of these eight components. Areas on which they need to focus may be the target of professional learning opportunities provided by the school or district, or by an external source. There are also many useful resources to consider for each of the eight components, depending on your level of implementation. (See, for example, DuFour, DuFour, Eaker, & Many, 2008.)

These eight steps are as follows (with the corresponding phase of the Design in Five process indicated in parentheses when applicable).

1. Establish and maintain a culture of collaboration.
2. Determine the priority standards (phase one).
3. Analyze the priority standards (phase two).
4. Plan a unit or quarter map (phase three).
5. Create or revise common summative assessments of the unit (phases four and five).
6. Create or revise common formative assessments (phases four and five).
7. Analyze the common assessment data and plan an instructional response (phase five).
8. Ensure students are integrally involved in their learning and in the assessment process (phase five).

Establish and Maintain a Culture of Collaboration

The school or collaborative teams have established a foundation for understanding the collaborative principles and have established norms for being and working together. They have successfully answered the following questions.

- What is the rationale and purpose for our work together?
- What do we expect of each other?
- How will we make decisions?
- How will we resolve conflict or disagreement?
- Do we understand how each member of our team best processes and communicates information?
- What do we believe about the contribution of each member?

Team members check in with each other regarding how they are functioning and perhaps reflect on the strengths of their collaborative work and how they might improve their collaborative culture to be even more productive.

Determine the Priority Standards

Each grade level, course, or content area has identified the priority or essential standards based on the following criteria (Ainsworth, 2003).

- **Endurance:** Are students expected to retain the skills or knowledge long after the test is completed?
- **Leverage:** Is this a skill or knowledge applicable to many academic disciplines?
- **Readiness for the next level of learning:** Is this skill or knowledge preparing the student for success in the next grade or course?

Collaborative teams plan their common formative and summative assessment work around these priority standards.

Analyze the Priority Standards

Collaborative teams analyze, or unpack, the priority standards to determine simple and complex learning goals that help guide the creation of assessments and give students an idea of all the steps (or parts) they need to achieve the priority standards. This is an essential aspect of building high-quality assessments. These learning goals direct the kinds of items and tasks on assessments. Phase two of the Design in Five process provides a more detailed protocol for this process.

As part of this step:

- The learning goals are turned into student-friendly statements (I can identify . . . I can explain . . . I can calculate . . . I can problem solve . . .)
- Learning goals are the foundation of the assessment plan
- Learning goals are clearly stated on assessments
- Students track their progress on these learning goals

Plan a Unit or Quarter Map

It is essential that collaborative teams have a curriculum map or plan that identifies the standards and learning goals to be taught during each unit or time frame to ensure students have an intentional curriculum and school experience. Collaborative teams also have a clear plan that articulates when they will use common formative assessments to plan interventions and responses to ensure that students will achieve the priority standards. A common assessment map describes the common formative assessments that your team will administer, analyze, and respond to in order to prepare students for the summative. The common assessment map (by quarter, unit, or year) also describes the common summative assessments that will reflect your students' learning of the priority standards. This map provides a plan of what evidence will be summative and what assessments will be practice, ensuring an intentional alignment between formative and summative assessment. This way, there are no surprises when students reach the point where they need to demonstrate their understanding.

Create or Revise Common Summative Assessments of the Unit

Summative assessments accurately reflect the level of thinking students have achieved. The summative measures the most essential learning goals of the priority standard. For these summative assessments:

- Rubrics and tasks are created that reflect the priority standards
- The test or task accurately reflects the learning goals intended
- The assessments have been reviewed for bias in terminology and design; every effort has been made to eliminate bias

Create or Revise Common Formative Assessments

The common formative assessments are smaller, shorter assessments that the team feels are essential to students being able to achieve the priority standard and that will prepare them for the summative assessment. There is a clear alignment between the thinking required in the summative assessment and the parts being assessed in the formative assessment. These common formative assessments are used to plan instructional responses. In the absence of an instructional response, this assessment will not be formative, but a summative snapshot.

Analyze the Common Assessment Data and Plan an Instructional Response

Collaborative teams analyze information from the common formative assessments (the actual numbers or student work). Teams bring the assessments to the table and stack them according to what students understand and what they misunderstand.

Based on these stacks or the data from a spreadsheet, teams plan a classroom or team response (a differentiated learning plan that all teachers then employ in their own classrooms; alternatively, each teacher takes one group of students at the same level of proficiency for a period of time to help them grow).

Collaborative teams check in to see the extent to which the response worked. Based on the results of the recheck, the team moves to the next learning goal or decides on an alternative plan to help all students achieve (this may mean trying another intervention or deciding to address it in a future unit). See the pile, stack, and plan process on page 115.

Ensure Students Are Integrally Involved in Their Learning and in the Assessment Process

In this final step, students are actively involved in gaining insight from their assessments. When students reflect on their assessments, beyond just a percentage, grade, or mark, they begin to make connections between their work and their learning. Phase five in Design in Five discusses in more detail the elements of getting students invested and involved. The following key practices provide a summary of the ways students can stay involved.

- Students track their progress on the learning goals or essential standards.
- Students reflect on what they understand and don't understand based on their assessment information; students then set goals and make plans as to how to take the next step toward achieving the standard.
- Students receive and act on descriptive feedback.
- Students offer descriptive feedback to peers.
- Students assess their own work.
- Students articulate what they are learning and where they are on their path.

Implement Collaborative Work: A Five-Step Protocol

Deep implementation of collaborative assessment practice that fosters a culture of learning requires the school leadership and collaborative teams to prioritize their work and intentionally plan why, when, and how that work will happen. Grade-level and content teams can use the following five-step protocol to determine how to best prioritize their collaborative work time during the school year.

1. Individual team members review each of the eight tasks and rate their own, their team's, or their school's work for each item using the scale shown in figure 6.2.

2. Share your individual ratings, come to some kind of consensus, and determine your priorities. Star a task or two that you feel are your strengths. This informs the tasks you include on your common assessment calendar (figure 6.1, page 110).

3. Circle a task or two that you feel your team may want to work on.

4. Decide on one or more of the tasks that your team may want to learn more about.

5. Plan your agenda (or sketch out tasks for a few meetings to plan ahead) and purpose (decide as a group what you want to accomplish). Remember to consider one of the most powerful aspects of collaborative work that influences learning is getting to the analysis of student work and the instructional plans that emerge from reviewing students' misconceptions in their work.

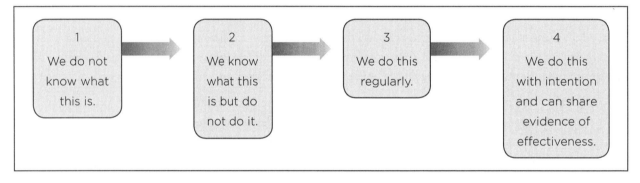

Figure 6.2: Scale for assessing and prioritizing assessment work.

Whether schools use these steps or create their own to describe the high-quality work of collaborative teams, it is essential that teachers reflect in the collaborative team meetings on student learning and respond to student needs in light of assessment information gathered. For another example of a framework describing the assessment work of collaborative teams, see page 144 or visit **go.solution-tree.com/assessment** to download a reproducible copy of "The Assessment Work of Teams."

Use Common Assessment Data

One of the most common questions posed during training sessions on common assessments is "How do we *efficiently* and *effectively* analyze and respond to the results of our common assessments?" Given the time constraints that often exist in the reality of school life, it is a compelling question. The analysis of student work and data is essential to help students learn at high levels.

Let's first consider *efficiency*. Sometimes schools have so much assessment data, it is hard to know where to begin. Teams of teachers collect assessment data frequently, but they don't intentionally plan any time to respond effectively. The end result is that educators have an intimate understanding of what needs work but don't spend the time or resources to address it. We keep assessing but don't stop to respond. Thus, teachers and students often feel like they are constantly being assessed with no time to slow down and learn. If we really intend to use common assessments to inform instruction, involve students, and improve achievement, just assessing more isn't going to do it. It will only add loads of paperwork to the already overwhelming role of teacher. What I call the "pile, stack, and plan" method is designed to help focus the analysis through stacking, versus extensive time scoring and recording data, in order to move quickly to an instructional plan that meets individual student needs.

Second, how can we be *effective*? Teachers may plan incredibly engaging and relevant lessons but wonder why students are making the same mistakes over and over again. Students, too, often point out how many different instructional activities they participate in throughout their day and struggle, sometimes, to find the connection between these activities and their learning.

To be effective, an assessment must help students grow in their understanding and improve their achievement and confidence. The timing must be right and instructional activity must be connected to their performance on the assessment. If the response is too far after the initial assessment, it may not connect or make sense to students and become another fragmented part of the day. Students need to see connections between their performance on an assessment and the instructional activity. What does this connectedness mean? It means that instructional responses to common assessment data include asking students to review and fix mistakes and to use comments to make improvements to their work. The assessment must tell students what they know or can do and what their next steps should be. A lesson plan includes time for students to work on the next steps either individually, with the teacher, in pairs, or in groups.

Pile, Stack, and Plan

This method has evolved through the exploration and experimentation of the teachers and teams with whom I have worked. The teams take a pile of student work; create stacks according to student understanding, common mistake, or misconception; and then design an instructional plan to meet students where they are in their understanding. The whole process should take about thirty to forty minutes—although the first time or two it may take a bit longer as teams explore this way of talking about student work.

1. Choose one learning goal—something you predict (or know) students often struggle with—and make sure it is essential for their success and worth spending more time on (for example, "I can draw conclusions from a data set").

2. Create a short common assessment to check understanding of this learning goal. This could be an exit slip, with students responding to one or two questions ten minutes before class ends, or part of a quiz, rough draft, or homework assignment that's already planned.

3. Bring actual student work (quizzes, exit slips, writing, and so on) to your team meeting. Review six to eight examples of the work, identifying strengths and misconception, or next steps that would improve the student's work. The team reviews each of these pieces of student work and then comes to consensus on strengths and next steps, or what these individual students need to work on.

4. Pile student work according to common mistakes or what they need to work on. Record those student names.

5. Plan instruction for each of those groups. Use figure 6.3 (page 116) to focus your work. The section Planning the Instructional Response on page 118 provides further guidance around what kind of instructional responses to consider.

6. When planning to use a short common assessment, consider when you will respond to the assessment information. Will you use the response plan the following week during literacy or math centers? Will you use it during the warm-up activity the day after you meet with

your team? Or will you use it to plan the next two to three days of instruction? Efficiency and effectiveness in this context are all about planning ahead and being intentional.

7. How will you check to see how effective the instructional response was? Will students submit a revision of their work? Will students do a short quiz or produce another piece of work to show their understanding after this response? Will the teacher do observations and make qualitative notes about any change in understanding?

8. When employing this process, consider the response and instructional planning from the common assessment part of your lesson planning (something you have to do anyway). If part of your assessment involves students self-assessing, where students identify their strengths and next steps based on their quiz or common assessment, use their self-reflection in your team meeting to plan an instructional response. All students with similar next steps will work together. The team plans an instructional activity or agenda for each group.

Learning Goal or Misconception to Work on:	Learning Goal or Misconception to Work on:	Learning Goal or Misconception to Work on:
Students:	Students:	Students:
Instructional Plan: 1. 2. 3.	Instructional Plan: 1. 2. 3.	Instructional Plan: 1. 2. 3.

Source: Adapted from Chapman & Vagle, 2011.

Figure 6.3: Instructional response planning form.

Visit **go.solution-tree.com/assessment** for a reproducible form of this figure and to see examples of instructional plans.

No matter how much time teachers have to analyze and respond to the data, I employ the one-third–two-thirds rule. One-third of the time is spent analyzing the data (pile and stack), and two-thirds of the time is spent on the instructional response (plan). I have noticed that teams spend most of their time analyzing student work, and in too many cases, meetings end with little or no time devoted to planning instructional responses. Planning new ways to help students understand is where tapping into the expertise of colleagues and sharing resources can be incredibly valuable. Here are some examples of potential common formative assessments to analyze.

- Math students' solutions to two math problems
- Science students' paragraphs on physical and chemical reactions
- Music students' identification of what made a rehearsal effective and ineffective
- Health students' responses to scenarios describing symptoms of diseases with their diagnoses and recommendations

Following are three examples using the pile, stack, and plan method, two involving math quizzes, and others involving examples of student writing.

The second-grade math team analyzed the results from their common formative assessment (see figure 4.12, page 71, second-grade money assessment). During a team meeting, teachers identified three areas. Students worked in one of the three stations based on how they performed on the assessment. The first group consisted of two students, and they struggled to identify the coins and their amounts. These students worked at a computer and watched a video describing through song the different coin amounts. They worked together to fix and revise their work on the actual quiz. The second group identified coins and their amounts. They needed to work on adding. These students played a game in which they practiced adding coins. They went back and fixed their adding errors after playing the game for about fifteen minutes. The final group performed well on all parts of the assessment. Their biggest struggle was to explain their thinking. This group also played a game, but it involved using what they knew about coins to solve problems posed on cards.

A middle school math team reviewed a quiz involving four problems on identifying slope and y-intercept. They stacked all students who accurately identified slope and y-intercept in one pile. Another pile contained students who could identify slope and y-intercept except when negative numbers were involved. The final pile held those students who had identified them all incorrectly. The team planned a twenty-minute station for each group to occur the following day in each of their classrooms. Each station had an agenda that teachers created based on how students performed on the assessment.

Another team brought examples of student writing to the meeting. They came to consensus on a strength and an area of growth for a few of the papers. Four growth areas were (1) replace repetitive words with more descriptive words, (2) develop an introduction that's more engaging, (3) work on run-on and fragment sentences, and (4) find more support for your main point. Teachers reviewed the rest of the student work, placing each piece in one of these growth areas. For those students who needed work on multiple areas, teachers chose one place for each of them to begin. It is too overwhelming (and de-motivating) for students to see all they need to work on at the same time.

The next day, the teachers offered a small minilesson on each of the areas, and the students received their papers back with their growth area identified. For the next thirty minutes, students worked independently to make revisions to their writing. Some teachers typed up the common comment and printed off as many copies as needed; this saved the time it would have taken to write on each paper.

The most challenging part of the process is planning the response and actually executing it. The trick is to use this process on something (a learning goal and assessment) that you had already planned to spend a few more days working on with students. This is only effective to the point that the response or intervention is actually executed. Another quick exit slip will tell you if the response was effective or if the next draft of their writing, lab report, or other work product indicates any improvement (see figure 5.8, page 96).

The following protocol will guide you through the process of instructional planning using the data from the pile, stack, and plan exercise.

First, you must answer the question, "What do we learn from the data?" Bring the actual student assessments (quizzes, writing, and so on) and data (item analysis, rubric scores) to the team meeting, organized by students, by classroom, and by learning goal. In analyzing the data, determine what the students' overall learning strengths and challenges are. Next, dig deeper and determine what each of the students needs to work on. There are several ways to go about this.

If you are analyzing a test with multiple items, you should first determine which items on the assessment are most essential. Of those items, which did students miss most often? Group the students by the errors they made on those items. For example, if the assessment is multiple choice, group all those who mistakenly chose A together and work with the team to decide why those students chose A. This will tell you what those students need to work on.

If you choose to view the assessment as a whole, group the students by misunderstandings. Pile and stack the actual pieces of student work by the mistakes made—that is, students who mastered the whole assessment (those who need challenge), students who missed a simple concept (basic inference), and students who understood the simple but missed something in the complex level (couldn't make a conclusion). With the team, decide what each group of students needs to work on next.

If you are looking at data that has been listed by learning goal on a template or grid, group students by the learning goal they need to improve. If students have multiple areas of need, choose one to make it manageable and attainable. Likewise, if you've used a rubric, group students by their scores on one criterion, the criterion they need to work on most.

Once you've determined what the students need to work on, take a look at the assessment itself and consider whether anything in the design of the assessment can explain students' errors. If so, revise the assessment accordingly.

The other question you need to ask is, "How do we respond to the data?" In answering this question, consider your instructional response and student investment. Use the template in figure 6.3 (page 116) to help guide your instructional response during which students are working on their next steps based on how they performed on the assessment. Consult the next section, Planning the Instructional Response, for more detailed information on effective responses. Regarding student investment, consider how the students are going to analyze their performance on the assessment. How will they learn from their mistakes?

You must also consider when and how the response will occur. Will the team respond individually within their classrooms? Will the students be divided into groups across the grade level? Will the response happen as a review before a test?

Finally, the team should check in regarding the impact of the response and discuss how to determine whether students have grown in their understanding and proficiency.

Planning the Instructional Response

In the pile, stack, and plan protocol, it is the planning that makes the students learn more. The planning of instructional responses is much like differentiating by readiness (Tomlinson, 1999), where students engage in activities based on evidence of what they need to understand and what they need to work on. There are considerations that make an instructional response, or differentiation by readiness, more effective. Differentiating instructional responses from formative assessment information means that collaborative teams or individual teachers analyze the student work or data from the assessment and determine what students understand and what they need to work on. From there, teams plan instruction to help students grow. Key aspects of differentiation from assessment information include *meeting students where they are*. From an assessment, identify student strengths (what they know based on evidence from the formative assessment) and what they need to work on (mistakes, errors, feedback). In addition, *plan instructional activities*. Instructional activities are based on our interpretations of the student work. Consider the following list of possible activities when creating an instructional response to formative assessment data.

- Students actively look at their work and figure out what they did wrong and make revisions.

- Students who need more explanation and a slower pace could perhaps use a podcast to walk them through the steps or the explanation as many times as they need.

- Students use feedback on papers to make revisions.

- Students summarize and take notes; teachers reinforce effort and provide recognition for improvement; students practice and use nonlinguistic representations; students engage in cooperative learning; teachers set objectives and provide feedback; students generate and test hypotheses, ask questions, act on cues, and use advance organizers (Marzano, Pickering, & Pollock, 2001).

- Teachers tap other instructional ideas from grade-level and content-specific resources.

Consider Resources Available

What kind of technology is available? Could a group of students watch a podcast or a video clip and then revise their work or complete another task? Are there other adults in the room that could help facilitate? What is the room space like? What kind of room design might aid in promoting effective instructional responses? You must also *consider structure*. Students can interact with the content, their peers, and the teacher in many different ways. Any given class can do well or not so well with a given structure. When deciding how to structure the instructional response, consider the following options, knowing that any one of them can be effective under the right conditions.

- Students participate in whole-class discussion.

- Students work individually. It may be that students get a task that they complete or work on individually. The task is based on their achievement on the assessment. One teacher provided an electronic assessment for students. As they finished their responses, she handed them an agenda based on how they worked the problems. Students independently worked on the task while the teacher walked around and helped students.

- Students work in small groups based on common areas of need. Before this is going to work well, clear guidelines about what's expected in the group are essential, such as how to engage in the group, what to do if you have a question, and how to communicate with the teacher throughout the session. The following two things help keep students engaged and on task: (1) a written agenda for each group explaining what they need to do step by step (some print this out for each group, others write it on a whiteboard or chart paper) and (2) a product or something they need to hand in either individually or as a group (sometimes students are revising their work or writing another draft).

- Students work at stations in pairs, individually, or in small groups.

- Students tap into existing routines, such as literacy centers, math stations, warm-up activities, and so on.

Consider Classroom Culture As Well

Another factor in the effectiveness of differentiation is the classroom culture. Consider the following.

- What are the classroom guidelines for collaboration with other students?

- How comfortable do students feel making mistakes and addressing them? Sharing their work? Getting feedback and using it to improve?

- Do students ask clarifying questions? Probing questions? High-level questions?

Consider Instruction Based on Readiness

Based on the work of Carol Ann Tomlinson (1999), John Hattie (2009), and Dylan Wiliam (2007), I have sketched out some ideas to consider based on three levels of readiness to learn. (Always be aware that readiness may vary and can be situational; readiness changes as students grow and learn.)

1. **Less-developed readiness** (the beginning stages of understanding). Teachers plan to:

    - Provide more direct instruction.

    - Use guided practice.

    - Use activities or products that are structured and concrete with fewer steps.

    - Guide students to bridge their own experience with the new (closer to their own experience).

    - Consider tasks that focus less on reading or require simpler reading skill.

    - Use deliberate pacing—more time to process.

    - Assess the situation—Are there students in this group who need the bigger picture about why this is important before they will grasp what they are not understanding?

    - Find ways to see help students see relevance and how the concept appears in context for the concept to click. For example, some kids may struggle with fractions—adding them or reducing them. Planning to have pizza with your class, however, might be a scenario they could relate to. In this example, teachers use fractions to represent how much pizza is left over.

    - If students are working in groups, begin with this group, those at the less-developed readiness, or in the beginning stages of understanding (while other groups have a step-by-step agenda they are following with the goal of completing something at the end of the time).

    - Explain the next step for students in a new way—with examples, video clips, or something different. For example, record short videos of you explaining the concept or ideas—a little lecture or you working a problem, revising writing, understanding a story or text. Allow students to watch it over as many times as they need to rework or revise their work. Post them online if possible or just give students access and time to view.

2. **More-developed readiness** (understand the basic concepts). Teachers plan to:

    - Provide descriptive feedback that students act on.

    - Ask students to review strong and weak examples of work and reflect on their own work in relationship to the examples.

    - Have students analyze mistakes and make revisions to the work. Students in this category understand the basic concept and can act more effectively on feedback to make those revisions.

    - Have students plan how to do it differently next time.

    - Ask students to make another attempt or do more practice on the concept in a new situation.

    - Have students create a step-by-step tip sheet about how to solve a problem, remember the concept, or describe the issue.

    - When working in groups, give students a step-by-step agenda of what to do. Be sure there is a product they need to create, an assessment they revise and submit either independently or as a group. These two ideas help a group stay on task without as much teacher guidance.

3. **Advanced readiness** (have mastered the concepts and need challenge and deeper extensions). Teachers plan to:

- Limit the amount of practice (or skip it all together) with skills and knowledge they have mastered.

- Engage students in activities and products that are more complex, open-ended, abstract, and multifaceted.

- Consider how the focus learning goal gets more complex. What does it look like when students are using these skills in authentic situations?

- Use a quick pace for simple skills and a slower pace with more complex tasks.

- Have students create items, tasks, or quizzes that are used as exit slips for other students.

- Have students revise their work and take it even deeper and then provide exemplars.

- Have students write letters to those making careers out of the subject (artists, mathematicians, engineers, authors, and so on) to ask questions, send these professionals work for feedback, or comment on something these professionals have written, created, or accomplished.

- Ask students to create a tip sheet for students to understand the concept—using visuals, instructions, and examples.

- Perhaps have these students work with other students. This is suggested with caution. Students in this group sometimes have a hard time working with students in the less-developed readiness category but can work really effectively with those in the more developed readiness stage. In addition, we want to use this only occasionally and be sure to push students in this group to deeper levels as well as giving them opportunities to help other students understand.

Assessment in collaboration has great potential to empower educators and help them grow in their own practice as well as contribute to the overall success of a school, team, and classroom. It is one of the most significant professional learning practices in which educators can engage. The protocols in this chapter can aid in promoting rich collegial conversations that lead to engaging assessment practices that inspire students to grow and invest in their learning.

Put Assessment in Collaboration Into Play

One essential aspect of implementation, or putting assessment collaboration in play, is clarity of purpose, scope, and use of assessment data. This is central to creating a culture of trust that promotes authentic conversations that empower teachers to support individual students in their learning. In Spring Lake Park, Minnesota, Jen Kunze and I worked with K–12 language arts, world language, mathematics, science, music, physical education, art, and social studies departments. Each group worked for two days to focus on assessment literacy and then, with our guidance, to craft summative assessments that reflected the rigor and expectations of the standard to ensure high expectations for students. The purpose statement shown in figure 6.4 (page 122) was refined and developed as the work continued to clearly communicate the importance of the work and how it was to be used.

What?

End-of-Trimester Common Assessment Purpose: The assessment is to provide evidence of students' achievement of the most critical ELO(s), or essential learning outcomes, of that term. It should reflect key ideas, not a culmination of everything taught.

Who Will Use the Data?

Teachers in PLCs and department meetings will use these data as reflection for teachers to consider their own practice in light of student work and achievement.

End-of-trimester common summative assessments will be used at the district level to understand how students are progressing toward being college ready (proficiency levels on this assessment are one data point among others that will be used to understand the extent to which students are on the path toward being college and career ready). This data is closer to the classroom than standardized tests and will provide another perspective on student achievement.

To ensure that what's being taught in the course is similar no matter who is teaching it and then also to ensure that there is a common piece of student work that reflects a certain level of proficiency in the ELOs.

Foundational Ideas About Common Assessments

- **Belief:** Assessment often drives what gets the most emphasis in instruction. What you inspect is what you expect. We are trying to do the right thing and care about our results. Being intentional about what that summative assessment is helps drive the instruction that is most meaningful and most essential.

- **Belief:** This type of assessment is different than standardized assessment—or autopsy data. This common assessment data is one piece of highly valid evidence to describe what students have achieved. The validity comes from intentionally aligning ELOs methods to develop a common summative assessment that the course is invested in.

- **Belief:** Common formative assessments are the work of a PLC, where we collectively support our students in learning more.

- **Belief:** Common summative assessments have the lofty goal of achieving equitable experiences for students while engaging in the work of a course. This means teachers will have the flexibility to design learning experiences in preparation for the common assessments.

Intention

Collectively come to agreement on the most important things in the course and emphasize them throughout our instruction. We intend to practice them throughout the trimester and have evidence (common summative assessment among others throughout the trimester) of students' proficiency.

Figure 6.4: End-of-trimester common assessment implementation plan.

Pause and Ponder

The following questions are designed to help individual teachers or teams focus on the essential ideas presented in this chapter.

- How would you define the purpose of common assessment work?

- How would you describe key aspects of effective common assessment practice?

- How does the Design in Five process support collaborative assessment work?

- If you have been implementing common assessment work, how clearly defined is the work? Is there a vision for the *why* of common assessments? To what extent are the collaborative teams invested in the work?

- How could some of the structures offered in this chapter provide guidance in deepening your common assessment work?

- Consider the eight components of collaborative assessment work. Using the Implement Collaborative Work protocol on page 113, assess your strengths and next steps to effectively improve your collaboration.

Epilogue: Building Hope

Assessment has the most amazing potential to inspire hope in students and empower teachers. At its best, assessment creates classrooms that foster the instinct to learn and grow. My hope is that the ideas in this book will help teachers design and use engaging assessments in ways that build students up and help them see possibility. Part of my own practice in supporting educators is always to welcome feedback—both the comments that help me understand how these ideas support your work and the comments that critique the work and make it better. As I type the last words on the page, there will be more experiences tomorrow that will make the work better, clearer, and more possible. It is in the journey and through the process that students and teachers create classrooms where learning is possible for all. Thank you for all you do to inspire children!

In closing, I leave you with a story that captures the frustration, excitement, possibility, grueling nature, and unending optimism that a journey to learn more about assessment promises. When my son Chase was four he was in an incredible preK classroom. Chase bounced everywhere, moved among groups of students easily, and cared about everyone's feelings (and could name his own). Chase didn't quite understand letters at this time and had little patience for writing—even his name. So, when an email from his teacher noted that "most kids in the class are writing and so please have your children write their friends' names on valentine cards"—two thoughts occurred to me: (1) he is way behind—yikes, and (2) how in the world is he going to write all of his friends' names when he can't recognize letters?

His teacher assured us that he was doing all of the things a prereader does, and the program he was in was not going to drill letter recognition into students but would make connections in natural and creative ways (which was a good fit for Chase). We chose this program for exactly that purpose. I am not one to drill these things with my children, as I know their frustration (and mine) will surely lead to a dread of reading and writing. We read and play games and sing the alphabet. I just gotta say, after the hundredth time of patiently identifying a C as a C and an S as an S to Chase, I was getting a bit concerned. We read books, and I'd say, "Do you recognize any letters?" And most often the answer was no—even when we had just talked about a particular letter. I didn't push it, but I was seriously contemplating flashcards.

There we were on Saturday before Valentine's Day, and I brought to the table a ton of patience and good intentions to remain calm. Chase and I began to write his valentine's cards; my plan was half today and half tomorrow. I wish I would have videotaped it. I wrote his name all in caps—CHASE—and together we said the letters. I pointed out where his name went (we had done this before, but it just didn't stick) and gave him a marker. He wrote the C. It might have been tipped on its side, which looked like the outline of a haystack, but the shape was there. He wrote H and then we got to A. He wanted the top to have a point, and his didn't. So, I held his hand, and together we made the point of an A. The S was curvy, really curvy, and the E was almost there with four horizontal lines facing backwards. But he wrote his name. On to the first of his friends' names. We discussed each letter of the first name, and then he wrote. I helped him a bit, and he asked questions to check in. We got back to writing his name—he got to A and looked up at me and asked, "What are we doing? What am I writing?" Patiently (OK, with gritted teeth), I reminded him we were writing his name. We got to the third name, and it had an *L* and an *E* and an *O*. He counted the letters and said, "Three— that's simple!" and he gave me a high five and started writing (not before the marker was on his face and all over his shirt because remember we're bouncing through this whole thing).

The next few names took thirty minutes, because after each one he would say something like, "That one looks good." I'd ask him why, and he'd respond with some characteristic of the letter. Then, sometimes he would say, "That's not good," and I'd ask, "What could we do to fix it?" He'd respond, and we'd make the fix either with my hand over his or with him writing independently. If I did too much, he would say, "No . . . no . . . no . . . I can do it," and proceed to write the letter on a scratch sheet of paper. He knew when he got it and when he didn't. He was frustrated when he felt overwhelmed—for example, when the name had a lot of letters (he would count each one of them) or unfamiliar letters. Chase would also start to shut down and say he didn't want to do it anymore if Mark (his dad) or I became impatient or he sensed (and he is a feeler) we were thinking it wasn't "right." Talk about a mirror—our reactions to his work directly influenced his degree of motivation.

A videotape of this experience might have tangibly captured, in action, assessment practices that are strength based and hope filled versus those that are deficit focused and punitively reinforced. If Chase perceived he couldn't do it or had an inkling that we thought he wasn't doing it, he resisted. When he knew what to do, when we broke it down into manageable chunks and pointed out ways that he was writing the letter, he persevered (and got really excited).

After five names, he was restless, so we called it quits. The next morning, as we are chatting, he asked out of the blue, "What's that letter, Mom, that has a straight line and three stripes?" I responded, "*E*," and he said, "Oh yeah, that's right!" Clearly, he was contemplating the letters. We wrote the rest of his friends' names and his own name.

The third morning, we started writing one of his teacher's names. "Look, Chase, Ms. Cori's name starts with same letter as yours." He responded, "Yes, what's that?" I stayed silent. He paused then said, "*C*." Wahoo! There were high fives all around.

Mark sat down with him, and they read each letter over and over again (maybe five times or more)—at Chase's request. Then, he exclaimed with absolute delight and satisfaction, "It's in my head now!" After about twenty-five more minutes of finishing up the last three cards, we were talking about playing letter games and just getting to know the letters better. Chase remarked with kind of a thoughtful yet hopeful attitude, "Well, I *definitely* know *C*!"

I was in one of those contemplative moods—soaking up each moment as Chase explored these letters through writing, stories, and cards. It's incredible to watch learning in action.

Engaging assessment practices foster hope and create a culture of learning when they build on strengths, see failure as opportunities to grow, patiently and relentless persist, and make tasks manageable and meaningful. Assessment practices have great potential to inspire students and teachers to see possibility and potential instead of feel dread and defeat. This journey is messy but well worth the time and effort. I wish you well!

Appendix: Reproducibles

The Design in Five Process

Phase One

1. Choose the standards.

2. Plan engagement.

Phase Two

1. Analyze the standards.

2. Sketch out the learning goals.

Phase Three

1. Identify the learning goals for the assessment.

2. Choose the method of assessment.

3. Determine the weight and number of items for each learning goal.

Phase Four

1. Create or revise assessment items and tasks for each learning goal.

2. Develop student documents and gather necessary materials.

Phase Five

1. Create a scoring scheme that reflects the learning.

2. Choose strategies to foster student investment.

Additional Resources

Understanding Learning Goals

- *Understanding by Design* (Expanded 2nd ed.), by Grant Wiggins and Jay McTighe

Creating Assessments

- *Common Core English Language Arts in a PLC at Work* series, edited by Douglas Fisher and Nancy Frey

- *Common Core Mathematics in a PLC at Work* series, edited by Timothy D. Kanold

- *High School Students: Practice Final Exams*—www.physicsforums.com/showthread .php?t=365673

- *Open-Response—How-To Tips*: http://newtonmathtutors.com/mcas/open -response-questions

- *Preparing 21st Century Students for a Global Society: An Educator's Guide to the "Four Cs"*: www.nea.org/assets/docs/A-Guide-to-Four-Cs.pdf

- *Teaching Students to Read Like Detectives: Comprehending, Analyzing, and Discussing Text*, by Douglas Fisher, Nancy Frey, and Diane Lapp

- *How to Assess Higher-Order Thinking Skills in Your Classroom*, by Susan M. Brookhart

Designing Assessments for Students With Special Needs

- Center on Standards and Assessment Implementation: http://csai-online.org

- National Alternate Assessment Center: www.naacpartners.org/Default.aspx

Designing Assessments That Are Culturally Relevant

- Cultural Infusion: http://culturalinfusion.org.au

- *Culturally Responsive/Relevant Teaching and Learning Resources*: www.husd.k12 .ca.us/SISP_CRTL

- Infusion of Culture: http://cultural-infusion.tumblr.com/

- An Introduction to Culturally Relevant Pedagogy [web log post]: www.tolerance.org/blog /introduction-culturally-relevant-pedagogy

Designing Assessments for English Learners

- Center for Authentic Intellectual Work: http://centerforaiw.com

- *Implementing RTI With English Learners*, by Douglas Fisher, Nancy Frey, and Carol Rothenberg

- "Informal Assessments for English Language Learners": www.colorincolorado.org /educators/assessment/informal/

Quality Grading and Reporting Practices Card

- *A Repair Kit for Grading: 16 Fixes for Broken Grades*, by Ken O'Connor

- *Classroom Assessment and Grading That Work*, by Robert J. Marzano

- *Developing Standards-Based Report Cards*, by Thomas R. Guskey and Jane Bailey

- *Grades That Mean Something: Kentucky Develops Standards-Based Report Cards*—www
.kentuckyteacher.org/wp-content/uploads/2011/11/Grades-that-mean
-something-article.pdf

- *Elements of Grading: A Guide to Effective Practice*, by Douglas Reeves

- *Formative Assessment and Standards-Based Grading*, by Robert J. Marzano

- *How to Grade for Learning: Linking Grades to Standards* (2nd ed.), by Ken O'Connor

- *On Your Mark: Challenging the Conventions of Grading and Reporting*, by Thomas R. Guskey

Differentiation Resources

- "Busting Myths About Differentiated Instruction": http://teachingss.pbworks.com/f
/BustingMythsaboutDI.pdf

- *Differentiated Instruction: Reaching All Students*: http://assets.pearsonschool.com/asset
_mgr/legacy/200916/MatMon092625HS2011Hall_20703_1.pdf

- *Differentiating Instruction for Advanced Learning in the Regular Classroom*: http://
researchhighachievers.wicomico.wikispaces.net/file/view/AACPS+Differentiated.pdf

- "Differentiated Instruction in the English Classroom: Content, Process, Product, and
Assessment" (sample chapter): www.heinemann.com/shared/onlineresources/E00577
/chapter4.pdf

- *Low Prep Strategies for Differentiating Instruction*: http://images.pcmac.org/SiSFiles
/Schools/TN/GreenevilleCity/GreenevilleHigh/Uploads/DocumentsCategories
/Documents/Low+Prep+DI+Strategiesnew.pdf

- *A Teacher's Guide to Differentiating Instruction*: www.centerforcsri.org/files/TheCenter
_NL_Jan07.pdf

Effective Collaboration Resources

- *Collaborating for Success With the Common Core: A Toolkit for Professional Learning
Communities*, by Kim Bailey, Chris Jakicic, and Jeanne Spiller

- *Common Formative Assessment: A Toolkit for Professional Learning Communities*,
by Kim Bailey and Chris Jakicic

Examples to Prompt Ideas

Example is not the main thing in influencing others. It is the only thing.

—Albert Schweitzer

Consistently educators ask, "What does this look like in practice? Do you have examples that can get me thinking?" I have collected and collected and collected. The amazing educators who deeply engage in professional dialogue and learning have graciously shared their work to provide concrete ways for their colleagues around the globe to talk about how to start or how to revise and deepen their assessment work. Visit **go.solution-tree.com/assessment** to find the following examples.

Examples Posted Online to Review and Consult	Context for the Examples
Analyzing Formative (Common and Individual) Assessment Student Work Protocol	This protocol was adapted from the pile, stack, and plan process as I worked with Ginnings Elementary School in Denton, Texas. This incredible group of educators planned a common formative assessment and brought the student work back to design an instructional response based on individual student learning needs. You will see examples of these responses following the assessments.
Kindergarten Math Common Formative Assessment Instructional Plan	JoAnn Rishel, Allison Nelson, Amy Wilhoit, Marlene Walker, and Nancy Bustos, kindergarten teachers at Ginnings Elementary School in Denton, Texas, crafted this instructional response plan from a common formative assessment using the analyzing common formative assessment protocol.
Kindergarten Math	This assessment was designed for a team wanting to experience a common formative assessment embedded into classroom instruction versus having to assess every student individually.
Kindergarten Reading	This sample kindergarten reading standard illustrates phases one, two, and three, where a standard is broken into learning goals, put into a ladder, and then used to create an accompanying assessment plan.
Race to 100	I designed this assessment for a team in Newfoundland, Canada, that wanted to use the game *Race to 100* as an assessment plan. Kindergarten and first-grade students used blocks to understand place value. This tracking sheet depicts the simple or complex learning goals (phase two). Teachers used this checklist to mark student understanding over the course of a couple of days (phase four). Then, the team reviewed where students were and planned their math groups for the next three days based on what target students needed to work on (phase five).
First-Grade Trimester One Math	This summative assessment was designed to capture how students are performing on learning goals after the first trimester. This was developed by Lisa Cisewski for three elementary schools in Spring Lake Park, Minnesota.

First-Grade Number Systems Learning Goals Ladder With Accompanying Assessment Plan and Sample Items	Brenda Fischer, Joylyn Gonzalez, and Joanna Meehan—first-grade teachers in South Sioux City Community Schools, Nebraska—developed this learning goal (phase two) and assessment plan (phase three) with accompanying items (phase four).
First-Grade Math Items by Cognitive Level	This example illustrates sample items for a mathematics standard by cognitive level.
Second-Grade Common Core Math: Phases One, Two, and Three	This second-grade example illustrates phases one, two, and three for a math standard.
Second-Grade Poetry	This second-grade assessment addresses standards related to poetry and is used to plan instruction from the student work the assessment generated.
Third-Grade Reading Items Per Cognitive Level Sample	This example illustrates sample items for a reading standard by cognitive level.
Third-Grade Language Arts Constructed-Response Sample	This is an elementary constructed-response sample.
Fourth-Grade Reading Per Cognitive Levels	This sample illustrates sample items for a fourth-grade reading standard by cognitive level that involves items around the learning goal "I can compare and contrast a first-hand and second-hand account."
Fourth-Grade Language Arts Summative Assessment Sample	This fourth-grade language arts assessment illustrates phases two, three, and four of the Design in Five process.
Fourth-Grade Equivalent Fractions Common Formative Assessment	This equivalent fractions common formative assessment was developed by Kimberly Lengerich in Denton, Texas. The student work informed an instructional response.
Fifth-Grade Reading	Renae Lemmons and her fifth-grade team in Denton, Texas, at Ginnings Elementary School, designed this assessment to help students learn more about reading and analyzing complex texts.
Seventh-Grade Reading Assessment	This seventh-grade reading assessment was adapted from the work of Kris Woolsey, a seventh-grade language arts teacher in Minnesota. It reflects phases two, three, four, and five of the Design in Five process.
Middle School Science	This example illustrates phases two, three, and four of the Design in Five process for a middle school energy standard.
Middle School Language Arts Constructed-Response Sample	This is a middle school language arts constructed-response sample.
Middle School Social Studies	This example was developed by Rachel Neckermann of Fort Zumwalt Schools, Missouri as a formative assessment that integrally involved students.
Middle School Art Rubric	This art rubric was designed by Julie Fahey in Spring Lake Park, Minnesota, as part of an end-of-trimester assessment.
Middle School Common Formative Assessment Protocol	This protocol was developed by a middle-school team of teachers from Cody Middle School in Cody, Wyoming and describes a series of questions to guide common formative assessment work at their school and to communicate the overall purpose of assessment practice—to support learning and high expectations.

Nuclear Chemistry	Phases one and two the Design in Five process are illustrated using this sample Texas chemistry standard, where a standard is broken down into learning goals and then put into a learning ladder.
Chemistry Assessment and Reflection of Results	This lab analysis was developed as the final in this course designed by a chemistry teacher in Spring Lake Park, Minnesota. Students did an item analysis of a final test, and the teacher used those individual lab analysis results to understand more clearly what had worked in her instruction and assessment practice and what she would focus on the following year.
Summative Geometry Test	Developed by Monica Carter and Tomi Pogact from Champlain Valley Union High School in Hinesburg, Vermont, this assessment clearly shows how rubrics can be used to score an assessment.
High School English	Beth Young designed this literary analysis of *The Things They Carried* (O'Brien, 2010). In this example, the task requires using text to support a claim. The combination of a checklist and rubric clearly outlines how the assessment will be graded (it is summative), and the rubric is used as feedback. Students are required to reflect on their own thinking about this particular list of items and to consider the rubric in a self-assessment of their writing.
World Language	This Spanish assessment was designed as an end-of-trimester assessment by Don Olson, Wendy Hatchner, Dan Buck, and Mike Miller in Spring Lake Park, Minnesota.
High School Health	Andrew Milne crafted this assessment, which was originally designed as multiple-choice items but turned into scenarios with more application. In addition, this assessment has a QR code which, when scanned, leads students to a website to view multiple videos that help them review for the test.
K–12 Writing Rubrics	These writing rubrics were designed over the course of one year. Each grade band met between three and eight times to develop the rubrics, use them, revise them, and collect exemplars. They are still being refined as teachers continually use them in deeper ways to inform instruction and develop a clear vision of writing proficiency from kindergarten all the way to twelfth grade.
Websites That Provide Resources for Assessment Design	Over the course of the last few years, I have facilitated numerous sessions around designing assessments. In some cases, I have built assessments alongside teachers or created them as models. I kept this list of websites by discipline and grade level as they were incredibly informative and helpful. I provide them to you as an example, knowing there will be many more websites that can inform your work.

Review Your Current Assessment With the Three Design Qualities

Use this template to determine how well your current assessments align with three design qualities synthesized from the work of many experts in this field: (1) designing with precision, (2) employing effective action, and (3) fostering student investment.

	Criteria	Yes	Somewhat	Unsure	No	Not Applicable
Designing With Precision	1. Are the learning goals clear?					
	2. Do the learning goals represent the most important goals for this particular assessment at this particular time?					
	3. Is there a mix of methods represented on the assessment, or is there a plan to provide students with the opportunity to show their understanding in multiple ways?					
	4. Is there a mix of cognitive levels? Does this assessment reflect the cognitive level required in the standard and does it capture the *why*?					
	5. Does the structure, layout, and setup of questions create the best possible conditions for students to show their understanding?					
	6. Are the directions present, and are they clear and concise? Does the visual layout of the assessment make it easy to understand and read?					
	7. If utilizing a technology tool, do students have the training needed to be able to use the tool in a meaningful way? Do they have access to and an understanding of what they need to utilize the tool?					
	8. Are the assessment questions or exercises written well—meaning, are they clear, succinct, and generally not confusing? Are they written in such a way that the answer to one question does not give away the answer to another?					
	9. Are the items written so they will provide information on students' strengths and weaknesses?					
	10. Is there anything in the assessment itself or in the conditions under which it would be administered that could lead to inaccurate estimates of student learning?					

page 1 of 2

Employing Effective Action	11. Are scores communicated to reflect learning?					
	12. If formative, is there a plan to provide students with descriptive feedback, to require revision, or to fix and learn from mistakes?					
	13. If summative, will students reflect upon the information from the assessment? Will they be able to identify their strengths and next steps based on the marks, grades, or rubric scores.					
Fostering Student Investment	14. Will the students identify strengths and next steps?					
	15. Will students make revisions to their work? Will students have the opportunity to create or produce work that shows higher achievement?					
	16. Will students set goals for future study?					
	17. Will students have opportunities to describe the extent to which they see this work as relevant and engaging, supportive (formative), or representative (summative) of their learning?					

Identify strengths of the assessment based on your answers to the design-quality checklist.

1.

2.

Identify revisions to the assessment based on your answers to the design-quality checklist.

1.

2.

Design in Five © 2015 Solution Tree Press • solution-tree.com
Visit **go.solution-tree.com/assessment** to download this page.

Assessment Beliefs Survey

To introduce and explore changing the culture of assessment, rate your agreement on the following five statements and then debate among colleagues the merits of the ideas and accompanying practices that would suggest your agreement or disagreement.

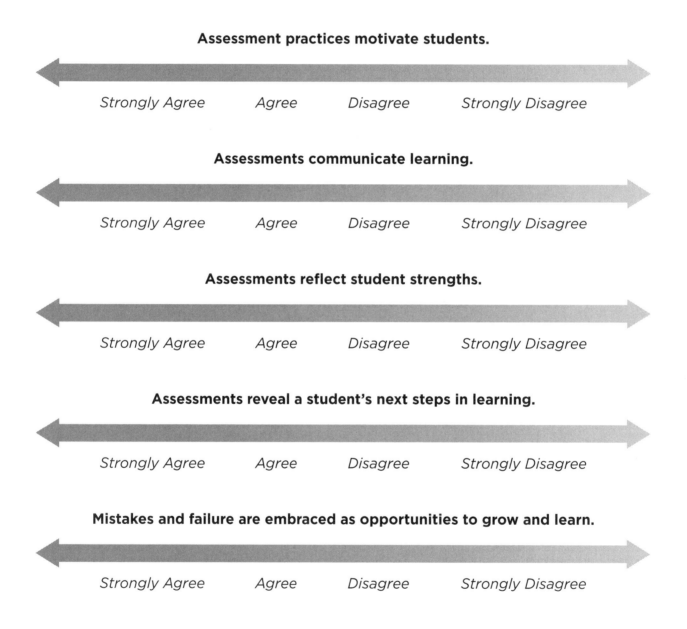

Assessment practices motivate students.

Strongly Agree   Agree   Disagree   Strongly Disagree

Assessments communicate learning.

Strongly Agree   Agree   Disagree   Strongly Disagree

Assessments reflect student strengths.

Strongly Agree   Agree   Disagree   Strongly Disagree

Assessments reveal a student's next steps in learning.

Strongly Agree   Agree   Disagree   Strongly Disagree

Mistakes and failure are embraced as opportunities to grow and learn.

Strongly Agree   Agree   Disagree   Strongly Disagree

Assessment Practice Strengths and Next-Steps Reflection

Use the following rating scale and reflection questions to create a picture of current assessment practices in your classroom, school, or district. Individual teachers, teams, or administrators may use this assessment to identify strength and growth areas.

Use the following confidence rating images to score the statements in the following table.

★　　I know what this is and do it regularly with intention.

✓　　I know what this is but haven't done much of it yet.

?　　I have questions about what this is and what it means.

Descriptive Statements of Assessment Practices	Confidence Rating	Next Steps
Clearly defined learning goals drive instruction.		
Clearly defined learning goals drive activities.		
Clearly defined learning goals drive assessments.		
Clearly defined learning goals drive grades or reporting practices.		
Assessment practices are balanced. Formative and summative practices are aligned and used intentionally.		
Students receive descriptive feedback that tells them what they know and what they need to do next.		
Students are invested in their learning (act on comments, use the information from their assessments to make revisions, analyze their mistakes, and set goals for their next steps in their learning).		
Assessments are designed well (accurate, free from bias, clear directions, valid, and reliable).		
Assessment data (common or individual) are analyzed to determine students' learning strengths and needs.		
Assessment data (common or individual) are used to plan instructional responses at the classroom or team levels (assessment data drives instruction—students are working on concepts based on what the data say).		
Assessment data inform teachers' instruction, curriculum, and assessment.		

page 1 of 2

Identify strengths: Based on your confidence ratings, what are the strengths of your assessment practice?

Set a goal or focus area: What do you want to learn more about or work on?

Check progress: Determine a few dates and times to check on your progress. This may be team meetings, department or grade-level meetings, staff meetings, or just dates that make sense in the rhythm of your work.

Date of Check-In	Progress How's it going? What's working? How do you know? What's challenging? Generate potential solutions.	Next Step

Phase One: Choosing Standards and Planning Engagement

Grade Level and Focus

Engagement Ideas

Standards

Notes

Phase Two: Learning Goals Ladder

Learning goals are what you will eventually target in the assessment. Once you have identified the learning goals, use this ladder to determine their level of complexity and rigor.

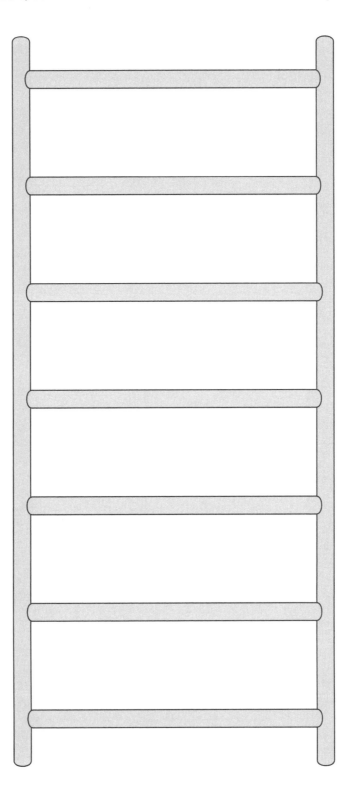

Phase Three: Assessment Plan Template

Once the simple and complex learning goals have been established, use this template to create an assessment plan that will connect the student work or method of assessment with the learning goals.

Learning Goals	Method	Weight	Total Number of Points

Phase Four: Assessment Tasks Per Cognitive Level

Use this template to match methods and items to the intended cognitive level required by a given standard.

Cognitive Levels	Methods	Sample Items, Tasks, and Prompts
Evaluation: *Appraise, argue, assess, attach, choose, compare, defend, estimate, judge, predict, rate, select, support, value, evaluate*	• Presentations • Projects • Scenarios	
Synthesis: *Arrange, assemble, collect, compose, construct, create, design, develop, formulate, manage, organize, plan, prepare, propose, set up, write*	• Presentations • Projects • Scenarios • Products • Plans	
Analysis: *Analyze, appraise, calculate, categorize, compare, contrast, criticize, differentiate, discriminate, distinguish, examine, experiment, question, test*	• Graphs • Essays • Projects • Scenarios	
Application: *Apply, choose, demonstrate, dramatize, employ, illustrate, interpret, operate, practice, schedule, sketch, solve, use, write*	• Essays • Some multiple choice • Plans • Storyboards	
Comprehension: *Classify, describe, discuss, explain, express, identify, indicate, locate, recognize, report, restate, review, select, translate*	• Short answers • Essays • Multiple choice	

Sample Common Assessment Weekly Calendar

Date	Task	Who	Expected Outcome
	• • •		
	• • •		
	• • •		
	• • • • Begin the cycle again.		

The Assessment Work of Teams

The following table describes the specific assessment tasks teams, or PLCs, do to focus on learning using evidence. The first column identifies concrete steps a team would employ. The second column aligns to key questions on which PLCs often focus their work. The third column describes concrete tasks in which teams engage. Team meeting agendas are informed by this list. The final column is a resource list to support teams in each step. Add your own people and resources to customize and align your assessment work to your context.

	Professional Learning Community Question (DuFour et al., 2008)	Tasks Your Team or PLC Does to Achieve This Step	Resources and People to Support This Work
Step 1: Identify the Key Learning	What is it we expect them to learn?	1. Identify the power, priority, or essential standards. 2. Analyze and deconstruct power standards to identify learning goals.	• Essential standard criteria • *Power Standards* by Ainsworth, 2003 • *Motivating Students* by Chapman and Vagle, 2011
Step 2: Map the Common Assessment(s) Plan	How will we know when they have learned it?	1. Identify and describe the summative assessment. 2. Plan formative assessments, or practice, that will be used before the summative to ensure students are prepared, are learning, and are growing.	• Design in Five
Step 3: Design and Administer the Assessment(s)	How will we know when they have learned it?	1. Agree on or create the summative assessment. 2. Agree on or create the common formative assessment(s).	• Design in Five • Student investment work (goal setting, tracking) • Data notebooks
Step 4: Analyze and Respond to Common Assessment Data	What will we do when they don't learn? What will we do when they do learn?	1. Gather the data, which could mean scores reported by students and learning goals on a spreadsheet, on chart paper, or the actual student work (quizzes, drafts, exit slips). 2. Use a protocol to understand the degree to which students demonstrated the intended learning. 3. Plan how you will respond (classroom, team, or school level).	• Pile, stack, and plan (analyzing common formative assessments) • Instructional-response ideas • Student-investment ideas

Design in Five © 2015 Solution Tree Press • solution-tree.com
Visit **go.solution-tree.com/assessment** to download this page.

References and Resources

Ainsworth, L. (2003). *Power standards: Identifying the standards that matter the most.* Englewood, CO: Advanced Learning Press.

Ainsworth, L., & Christinson, J. (1998). *Student-generated rubrics: An assessment model to help all students succeed.* Orangeburg, NY: Seymour.

Ainsworth, L., & Viegut, D. (2006). *Common formative assessments: How to connect standards-based instruction and assessment.* Thousand Oaks, CA: Corwin Press.

Alkharusi, H. (2013). Canonical correlational models of students' perceptions of assessment tasks, motivational orientations, and learning strategies. *International Journal of Instruction, 6*(1), 21–38.

Allensworth, E., Correa, M., & Ponisciak, S. (2008, May). *From high school to the future: ACT preparation—Too much, too late.* Chicago: Consortium on Chicago School Research at the University of Chicago.

Amrein, A. L., & Berliner, D. C. (2003). The effects of high-stakes testing on student motivation and learning. *Educational Leadership, 60*(5), 32–38.

Arter, J. A., & Busick, K. U. (2001). *Practice with student-involved classroom assessment: A workbook and learning team guide.* Portland, OR: Assessment Training Institute.

Arter, J. A., & McTighe, J. (2001). *Scoring rubrics in the classroom: Using performance criteria for assessing and improving student performance.* Thousand Oaks, CA: Corwin Press.

Arter, J. A., & Nutting, B. (1998). *Student assessment mini-lessons for your staff.* Portland, OR: Northwest Regional Educational Laboratory.

Arter, J. A., Stiggins, R. J., Duke, D., & Sagor, R. (1993). Promoting assessment literacy among principals. *NASSP Bulletin, 77*(556), 1–7.

Assidere. (2014): In *Latdict.* Accessed at www.latin-dictionary.net/definition/5139/assideo-assidere-assedi-assessus on December 12, 2012.

Bailey, K. Jakicic, C., & Spiller, J. (2013). *Collaborating for success with the Common Core: A toolkit for professional learning communities at work.* Bloomington, IN: Solution Tree Press.

Beers, S. Z. (2011). *Teaching 21st century skills: An ASCD action tool.* Alexandria, VA: Association for Supervision and Curriculum Development.

Bellanca, J. A., Fogarty, R. J., & Pete, B. M. (2012). *How to teach thinking skills within the Common Core: 7 key student proficiencies of the new national standards.* Bloomington, IN: Solution Tree Press.

Belsky, S. (2013, August 30). Accept the burden of processing uncertainty [Web log post]. Accessed at http://t.co/8HLlE7INhJ on January 20, 2014.

Black, P., & Wiliam, D. (1998). Assessment and classroom learning. *Assessment in Education: Principles, Policy and Practice, 5*(1), 7–74.

Black, P., Harrison, C., Lee, C., Marshall, B., & Wiliam, D. (2002). *Working inside the black box: Assessment for learning in the classroom.* London: King's College.

Bonner, S. M. (2013). Validity in classroom assessment: Purposes, properties, and principles. In J. H. McMillan (Ed.), *Handbook of research on classroom assessment* (pp. 87–106). Thousand Oaks, CA: SAGE.

Brookhart, S. M. (2013a). Classroom assessment in the context of motivation theory and research. In J. H. McMillan (Ed.), *Handbook of research on classroom assessment* (pp. 35–54). Thousand Oaks, CA: SAGE.

Brookhart, S. M. (2013b). *How to create and use rubrics for formative assessment and grading.* Alexandria, VA: Association for Supervision and Curriculum Development.

Burton, S. J., Sudweeks, R. R., Merrill, P. F., & Wood, B. (1991). *How to prepare better multiple-choice test items: Guidelines for university faculty.* Provo, UT: Brigham Young University Testing Services.

Butler, R. (1988). Enhancing and undermining intrinsic motivation: The effects of task-involving and ego-involving evaluation on interest and performance. *British Journal of Educational Psychology, 58*(1), 1–14.

Carr, J. F., & Harris, D. E. (2001). *Succeeding with standards: Linking curriculum, assessment, and action planning.* Alexandria, VA: Association for Supervision and Curriculum Development.

Center for the Study of the American Dream. (2014). *Annual State of the American Dream Survey.* Cincinnati, OH: Xavier University. Accessed at www.xavier.edu/americandream/programs/survey.cfm on April 15, 2014.

Chapman, C., & Vagle, N. (2011). *Motivating students: 25 strategies to light the fire of engagement.* Bloomington, IN: Solution Tree Press.

Chappuis, J. (2009). *Seven strategies of assessment FOR learning.* Princeton, NJ: Educational Testing Service.

Chappuis, J., & Chappuis, S. (2002). *Understanding school assessment: A parent and community guide to helping students learn.* Portland, OR: Assessment Training Institute.

Chappuis, S., & Stiggins, R. J. (2002). Classroom assessment for learning. *Educational Leadership, 60*(1), 40–43.

Chappuis, S., Stiggins, R. J., Arter, J., & Chappuis, J. (2004). *Assessment for learning: An action guide for school leaders* (2nd ed.). Portland, OR: Assessment Training Institute.

Council for Aid to Education. (2014). *CLA+ overview.* Accessed at http://cae.org/performance-assessment/category/cla-overview on May 17, 2014.

Cruickshank, D. R., Jenkins, D. B., & Metcalf, K. K. (2006). *The act of teaching* (4th ed.). Boston: McGraw-Hill.

Davidson, C. N. (2011). *Now you see it: How the brain science of attention will transform the way we live, work, and learn.* London: Penguin.

Davies, A. (2007a). Involving students in the classroom assessment process. In D. B. Reeves (Ed.), *Ahead of the curve: The power of assessment to transform teaching and learning* (pp. 31–58). Bloomington, IN: Solution Tree Press.

Davies, A. (2007b). *Making classroom assessment work* (2nd ed.). Courtenay, Canada: Building Connections.

Deevers, M. (2006, April). *Linking classroom assessment practices with student motivation in mathematics.* Paper presented at the annual meeting of the American Educational Research Association, San Francisco.

Dietel, R. J., Herman, J. L., & Knuth, R. A. (1991). *What does research say about assessment?* Oak Brook, IL: North Central Regional Educational Laboratory. Accessed at http://methodenpool.uni-koeln.de/portfolio/What%20Does%20Research%20Say%20About%20Assessment.htm on July 28, 2014.

Dooms, M. (2012, August 15). Standards based grading in a percentage based world [Web log post]. Accessed at http://teacherleaders.wordpress.com/2012/08/15/standards-based-grading-in-a-percentage-based-world/ on April 16, 2014.

DuFour, R., DuFour, R., & Eaker, R. (2008). *Revisiting professional learning communities at work: New insights for improving schools.* Bloomington, IN: Solution Tree Press.

DuFour, R., DuFour, R., Eaker, R., & Karhanek, G. (2004). *Whatever it takes: How professional learning communities respond when kids don't learn.* Bloomington, IN: Solution Tree Press.

DuFour, R., & Eaker, R. (1998). *Professional learning communities at work: Best practices for enhancing student achievement.* Bloomington, IN: Solution Tree Press.

DuFour, R., Eaker, R., & DuFour, R. (Eds.). (2005). *On common ground: The power of professional learning communities.* Bloomington, IN: Solution Tree Press.

Dunn, K. E., & Mulvenon, S. W. (2009). A critical review of research on formative assessment: The limited scientific evidence of the impact of formative assessment in education. *Practical Assessment, Research and Evaluation, 14*(7), 1–11.

Dweck, C. S. (2006). *Mindset: The new psychology of success.* New York: Ballantine Books.

EdLeader21. (2012). *The PLC: EdLeader21.* Accessed at www.edleader21.com/index.php?pg=2 on April 14, 2014.

Erkens, C. (2013). *Building common assessments* [Training materials]. Bloomington, IN: Solution Tree Press.

Fisher, D., Frey, N., & Rothenberg, C. (2011). *Implementing RTI with English learners.* Bloomington, IN: Solution Tree Press.

Fitzgerald, F. S. (1926). Winter dreams. In *All the sad young men.* New York: Scribner's Sons.

Forehand, M. (2005). Bloom's taxonomy: In M. Orey (Ed.), *Emerging perspectives on learning, teaching, and technology.* Accessed at http://projects.coe.uga.edu/epltt on May 16, 2014.

Gallas, K. (1994). *The languages of learning: How children talk, write, dance, draw, and sing their understanding of the world.* New York: Teachers College Press.

Gareis, C. R., & Grant, L. W. (2008). *Teacher-made assessments: How to connect curriculum, instruction, and student learning.* Larchmont, NY: Eye on Education.

Garmston, R. S., & Wellman, B. M. (1999). *The adaptive school: A sourcebook for developing collaborative groups.* Norwood, MA: Christopher-Gordon.

Gay, G. (2002). Preparing for culturally responsive teaching. *Journal of Teacher Education, 53*(2), 106–116.

Gregory, K., Cameron, C., & Davies, A. (2011). *Self-assessment and goal setting* (2nd ed.). Bloomington, IN: Solution Tree Press.

Gullickson, A. R. (2003). *The student evaluation standards: How to improve evaluations of students.* Thousand Oaks, CA: Corwin Press.

Guo, Y., Connor, C. M., Yang, Y., Roehrig, A. D., & Morrison, F. J. (2012). The effects of teacher qualification, teacher self-efficacy, and classroom practices on fifth graders' literacy outcomes. *Elementary School Journal, 113*(1), 3–24.

Guskey, T. R. (2002). *How's my kid doing?: A parent's guide to grades, marks, and report cards.* San Francisco: Jossey-Bass.

Guskey, T. R. (2015). *On your mark: Challenging the conventions of grading and reporting.* Bloomington, IN: Solution Tree Press.

Guskey, T. R., & Bailey, J. M. (2001). *Developing grading and reporting systems for student learning.* Thousand Oaks, CA: Corwin Press.

Guskey, T. R., & Bailey, J. M. (2010). *Developing standards-based report cards.* Thousand Oaks, CA: Corwin Press.

Hanushek, E. A. (2011). Valuing teachers: How much is a good teacher worth? *Education Next, 11*(3), 40–45.

Harris, F. (2009). *Untitled.* Unpublished manuscript.

Hattie, J. A. C. (2003). *Teachers make a difference: What is the research evidence?* Camberwell, Victoria, Australia: Australian Council for Educational Research. Accessed at www.acer.edu.au/documents/RC2003_Hattie_TeachersMakeADifference.pdf on December 19, 2012.

Hattie, J. A. C. (2009). *Visible learning: A synthesis of over 800 meta-analyses relating to achievement.* Cambridge, MA: Routledge.

Hattie, J. A. C., & Timperley, H. (2007). The power of feedback. *Review of Educational Research, 77*(1), 81–112.

Henderson, N. (2013). Havens of resilience. *Educational Leadership, 71*(1), 22–27.

Hess, K. K. (2006). *Exploring cognitive demand in instruction and assessment.* Accessed at http://secondaryinstruction.muscogee.k12.ga.us/InstructionalSupport/DOK_ApplyingWebb_KH08%20Levels%20of%20Cognitive%20Demand%20p5.pdf on May 16, 2014.

Hollie, S. (2008). *Using culturally and linguistically responsive teaching to enhance learning for all students.* Boston: Pearson Longman.

ikleyn. (n.d.). *Lesson using quadratic equations to solve word problems.* Accessed at www.algebra.com/algebra/homework/quadratic/lessons/Using-quadratic-equations-to-solve-word-problems.lesson on April 16, 2014.

Lattimer, H. (2008). Challenging history: Essential questions in the social studies classroom. *Social Education, 72*(6), 326–329. Accessed at http://bit.ly/XNcXZD on January 20, 2014.

Lehmann, I. J., & Mehrens, W. A. (1987). Using teacher-made measurement devices. *NASSP Bulletin, 71*(496), 36–44.

Lehner, C. (2013, June 7). Communication tools [Web log post]. Accessed at http://iamateacher-thisismyjourney.blogspot.ca/2013/06/communication-tools.html on April 16, 2014.

Linn, A. (2013). The state of the American dream is uncertain. *NBC News.* Accessed at www.nbcnews.com/business/economy/state-american-dream-uncertain-f6C10508356 on April 15, 2014.

Little, J. L., Bjork, E. L, Bjork, R. A., & Angello G. (2012). Multiple-choice tests exonerated, at least of some of the charges: Fostering test-induced learning and avoiding test-induced forgetting. *Journal of Psychological Science, 23*(11), 1337–1344.

Martin, A. J. (2008). Enhancing student motivation and engagement: The effects of a multidimensional intervention. *Contemporary Educational Psychology, 33*(2), 239–269.

Marzano, R. J. (2000). *Transforming classroom grading.* Alexandria, VA: Association for Supervision and Curriculum Development.

Marzano, R. J. (2003). *What works in schools: Translating research into action.* Alexandria, VA: Association for Supervision and Curriculum Development.

Marzano, R. J. (2006). *Classroom assessment and grading that work.* Alexandria, VA: Association for Supervision and Curriculum Development.

Marzano, R. J. (2007). *The art and science of teaching: A comprehensive framework for effective instruction.* Alexandria, VA: Association for Supervision and Curriculum Development.

Marzano, R. J. (2010). *Formative assessment & standards-based grading.* Bloomington, IN: Marzano Research Laboratory.

Marzano, R. J., & Kendall, J. S. (2007). *The new taxonomy of educational objectives* (2nd ed.). Thousand Oaks, CA: Corwin Press.

McDonald, J. P., Mohr, N., Dichter, A., & McDonald, E. (2003). *The power of protocols: An educator's guide to better practice.* New York: Teachers College Press.

McMillan, J. H. (2013). Why we need research on classroom assessment. In J. H. McMillan (Ed.), *Handbook of research on classroom assessment* (pp. 3–16). Thousand Oaks, CA: SAGE.

McTighe, J., & Wiggins, G. (2013). *Essential questions: Opening doors to student understanding.* Alexandria, VA: Association for Supervision and Curriculum Development.

Mongare, G. (2009). *Teaching experience.* Unpublished manuscript.

Moore, J. (2011). *Freckleface Strawberry: Best friends forever.* New York: Bloomsbury.

Moss, C. M. (2013). Research on classroom summative assessment. In J. H. McMillan (Ed.), *Handbook of research on classroom assessment* (pp. 235–256). Thousand Oaks, CA: SAGE.

National Education Association. (2003). *Balanced assessment: The key to accountability and improved student learning.* Washington, DC: Author.

National Governors Association Center for Best Practices & Council of Chief State School Officers. (2010a). *Common Core State Standards for English language arts and literacy in history/social science, science, & technical subjects.* Washington, DC: Authors. Accessed at www.corestandards.org/assets/CCSSI_ELA percent20Standards.pdf on July 29, 2014.

National Governors Association Center for Best Practices & Council of Chief State School Officers. (2010b). *Common Core State Standards for mathematics.* Washington, DC: Authors. Accessed at www.corestandards.org/assets/CCSSI _Math percent20Standards.pdf on July 29, 2014.

Newmann, F. M., King, M. B., & Carmichael, D. L. (2007). *Authentic instruction and assessment: Common standards for rigor and relevance in teaching academic subjects.* Des Moines: Iowa Department of Education.

Oates, J. C. (1973). Dreaming America. In *Dreaming America & other poems.* New York: Aloe Editions.

Oates, J. C. (1997, May 20). *Joyce Carol Oates interview for National Book Award.* Accessed at www.achievement.org /autodoc/page/oat0int-5 on May 17, 2014.

O'Brien, T. (2010). *The things they carried.* New York: Mariner Books.

O'Connor, K. (2002). *How to grade for learning: Linking grades to standards* (2nd ed.). Thousand Oaks, CA: Corwin Press.

O'Connor, K. (2008). *A repair kit for grading: 15 fixes for broken grades.* Portland, OR: Educational Testing Service.

O'Connor, K. (2011). *A repair kit for grading: 15 fixes for broken grades* (2nd ed.). Boston: Pearson.

Parkes, J. (2013). Reliability in classroom assessment. In J. H. McMillan (Ed.), *Handbook of research on classroom assessment* (pp. 107–124). Thousand Oaks, CA: SAGE.

Pfeffer, J., & Sutton, R. I. (2000). *The knowing-doing gap: How smart companies turn knowledge into action.* Boston: Harvard Business School Press.

Popham, W. J. (2001). *The truth about testing: An educator's call to action.* Alexandria, VA: Association for Supervision and Curriculum Development.

Popham, W. J. (2003). *Test better, teach better: The instructional role of assessment.* Alexandria VA: Association for Supervision and Curriculum Development.

Popham, W. J. (2005). *Classroom assessment: What teachers need to know* (4th ed.). Boston: Pearson.

Reeves, D. B. (2004a). *101 more questions & answers about standards, assessment, and accountability.* Denver, CO: Advanced Learning Press.

Reeves, D. B. (2004b). *Accountability for learning: How teachers and school leaders can take charge.* Alexandria VA: Association for Supervision and Curriculum Development.

Reeves, D. B. (Ed.). (2007). *Ahead of the curve: The power of assessment to transform teaching and learning.* Bloomington, IN: Solution Tree Press.

Reeves, D. B. (2011). *Elements of grading: A guide to effective practice.* Bloomington, IN: Solution Tree Press.

Rodgers, C. R. (2006). Attending to student voice: The impact of descriptive feedback on learning and teaching. *Curriculum Inquiry, 36*(2), 209–237.

Rodriguez, M. C. (2004). The role of classroom assessment in student performance on TIMSS. *Applied Measurement in Education, 17*(1), 1–24.

Rossetti, C. (1947). Who has seen the wind? In J. W. Watson (Ed.), *The Golden book of poetry*. New York: Simon & Schuster. Accessed at www.poetryfoundation.org/poem/171952 on July 23, 2014.

Rudner, L. M., & Schafer, W. D. (2002). *What teachers need to know about assessment*. Washington, DC: National Education Association.

Sadler, D. R. (1989). Formative assessment and the design of instructional systems. *Instructional Science, 18*, 119–144.

Sadler, D. R. (2008). Formative assessment and the design of instructional systems. In W. Harlan (Ed.), *Student assessment and testing* (pp. 3–28). London: SAGE.

Schlechty, P. C. (2011). *Engaging students: The next level of working on the work*. San Francisco: Jossey-Bass.

Schmoker, M. (2011). *Focus: Elevating the essentials to radically improve student learning*. Alexandria, VA: Association for Supervision and Curriculum Development.

Schulte, M. (2009). *Making a difference*. Unpublished manuscript.

Schwartz, M. (2011). Dots in blue water [Web log post]. Accessed at www.dotsinbluewater.com/about.html on May 28, 2014.

Seider, S., Gilbert, J. K., Novick, S., & Gomez, J. (2013). The role of moral and performance character strengths in predicting achievement and conduct among urban middle school students. *Teachers College Record, 115*(8), 1–34. Accessed at www.tcrecord.org/Content.asp?ContentId=17075 on January 21, 2014.

Shepard, L. A. (2000). The role of assessment in a learning culture. *Educational Researcher, 29*(7), 4–14.

Shepard, L., Hammerness, K., Darling-Hammond, L., & Rust, F. (2005). Assessment. In L. Darling-Hammond & J. Bransford (Eds.), *Preparing teachers for a changing world: What teachers should learn and be able to do* (pp. 275–326). San Francisco: Jossey-Bass.

Snow, E., Fulkerson, D., Feng, M., Nichols, P., Mislevy, R., & Haertel, G. (2010, March). *Leveraging evidence-centered design in large-scale test development (Large-scale assessment technical report 4)*. Menlo Park, CA: SRI International.

Springen, K. (2013, June). *Cancer's big questions*. Accessed at www.pageturnpro.com/Publications/201305/1812/50784/pdf/130136372715682522_Cancer.pdf on January 21, 2014.

Stiggins, R. J. (2002). Assessment crisis: The absence of assessment for learning. *Phi Delta Kappan, 83*(10), 758–765.

Stiggins, R. J. (2005). *Student-involved assessment for learning* (4th ed.). Upper Saddle River, NJ: Merrill/Prentice Hall.

Stiggins, R. J., Arter, J. A., Chappuis, J., & Chappuis, S. (2004). *Classroom assessment for student learning: Doing it right, using it well*. Portland, OR: Assessment Training Institute.

Swift, T., Martin, M., & Shellback. (2012). I knew you were trouble [Recorded by Taylor Swift]. On *Red* [CD]. Nashville, TN: Big Machine Records.

Tepper, S. J., & Kuh, G. D. (2011, September 4). Let's get serious about cultivating creativity. *Chronicle Review, 58*(3), B13–B14. Accessed at http://chronicle.com/article/Lets-Get-Serious-About/128843/ on January 21, 2014.

Tomlinson, C. A. (1999). *The differentiated classroom: Responding to the needs of all learners*. Alexandria VA: Association for Supervision and Curriculum Development.

Vagle, N. M. (2008, July 7). Moving beyond super job: Descriptive feedback that inspires and requires action [Web log post]. Accessed at www.allthingsassessment.info/wordpress/?p=55 on January 21, 2014.

Vagle, N. M. (2009a). Finding meaning in the numbers. In T. R. Guskey (Ed.), *The principal as assessment leader* (pp. 149–173). Bloomington, IN: Solution Tree Press.

Vagle, N. M. (2009b). Inspiring and requiring action. In T. R. Guskey (Ed.), *The teacher as assessment leader* (pp. 203–225). Bloomington, IN: Solution Tree Press.

Walvoord, B. E., & Anderson, V. J. (1998). *Effective grading: A tool for learning and assessment.* San Francisco: Jossey-Bass.

Whitman, W. (1860). I hear America singing. In *Leaves of grass.* Boston: Rand & Avery.

Wiggins, G. (1998). *Educative assessment: Designing assessments to inform and improve student performance.* San Francisco: Jossey-Bass.

Wiggins, G., & McTighe, J. (2005). *Understanding by design* (Expanded 2nd ed.). Alexandria, VA: Association for Supervision and Curriculum Development.

Wiliam, D. (2011). *Embedded formative assessment.* Bloomington, IN: Solution Tree Press.

Wiliam, D. (2013, June). *How do we prepare students for a world we cannot imagine?* Speech presented at the Minnetonka Institute for Leadership, Minnetonka, Minnesota.

Wiliam, D., Lee, C., Harrison, C., & Black, P. (2004). Teachers developing assessment for learning: Impact on student achievement. *Assessment in Education: Principles, Policy and Practice, 11*(1), 49–65.

Wineburg, S., & Schneider, J. (2009). Inverting Bloom's taxonomy. *Education Week, 29*(6), 28–29, 31.

Wininger, S. R. (2005). Using your tests to teach: Formative summative assessment. *Teaching of Psychology, 32*(3), 164–166.

Wisconsin Center of Education Research—University of Wisconsin-Madison. (n.d.). *Web alignment tool.* Madison: Author. Accessed at www.wcer.wisc.edu/WAT/index.aspx on January 21, 2014.

Worthen, B. R., Borg, W. R., & White, K. R. (1993). *Measurement and evaluation in the schools.* New York: Longman.

Xu, Y. (2013). Classroom assessment in special education. In J. H. McMillan (Ed.), *Handbook of research on classroom assessment* (pp. 431–448). Thousand Oaks, CA: SAGE.

Yacob, H. (2009). *Teaching.* Unpublished manuscript.

Ziegler, D. (2008). Relevance in education? *Evolution: Education and Outreach, 1*(4), 517–519.

Index

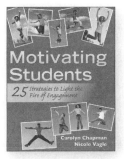

Motivating Students: 25 Strategies to Light the Fire of Engagement
By Carolyn Chapman and Nicole Dimich Vagle

Learn why students disengage and how to motivate them to achieve success with a five-step framework. Research-based strategies and fun activities, along with tips and troubleshooting advice, show how to instill a lasting love of learning in students of any age.

BKF371

Common Formative Assessment: A Toolkit for Professional Learning Communities at Work™
By Kim Bailey and Chris Jakicic

The catalyst for real student improvement begins with a decision to implement common formative assessments. In this conversational guide, the authors offer tools, templates, and protocols to incorporate common formative assessments into the practices of a PLC to monitor and enhance student learning.

BKF538

The Teacher as Assessment Leader
Edited by Thomas R. Guskey
By Cassandra Erkens, William M. Ferriter, Michelle Goodwin, Tammy Heflebower, Tom Hierck, Chris Jakicic, Sharon V. Kramer, Jeffry Overlie, Ainsley B. Rose, Nicole Dimich Vagle, and Adam Young

Meaningful examples, expert research, and real-life experiences illustrate the capacity and responsibility every educator has to ignite positive change. Packed with practical strategies for designing, analyzing, and using assessments, this book shows how to turn best practices into usable solutions.

BKF345

The Principal as Assessment Leader
Edited by Thomas R. Guskey
By Cassandra Erkens, William M. Ferriter, Tammy Heflebower, Tom Hierck, Charles Hinman, Susan B. Huff, Chris Jakicic, Dennis King, Ainsley B. Rose, Nicole Dimich Vagle, and Mark Weichel

Filled with firsthand experiences from expert practitioners, this book delivers the motivation needed to ignite a shift toward formative assessment and overall school improvement. Topics include building teacher literacy, providing targeted professional development, acquiring appropriate technology, and more.

BKF344

Embedded Formative Assessment
By Dylan Wiliam

Emphasizing the instructional side of formative assessment, this book explores in depth the use of classroom questioning, learning intentions and success criteria, feedback, collaborative and cooperative learning, and self-regulated learning to engineer effective learning environments for students.

BKF418